Access 2003:
Basic
Student Manual

Access 2003: Basic

VP and GM of Courseware:	Michael Springer
Series Product Managers:	Charles G. Blum and Adam A. Wilcox
Developmental Editor:	Don Tremblay
Keytesters:	Michele Jacobson and Bill Bateman
Series Designer:	Adam A. Wilcox
Cover Designer:	Abby Scholz

COPYRIGHT © 2006 Course Technology, a division of Thomson Learning. Thomson Learning is a trademark used herein under license.

ALL RIGHTS RESERVED. No part of this work may be reproduced, transcribed, or used in any form or by any means—graphic, electronic, or mechanical, including photocopying, recording, taping, Web distribution, or information storage and retrieval systems—without the prior written permission of the publisher.

For more information contact:

Course Technology
25 Thomson Place
Boston, MA 02210

Or find us on the Web at: www.course.com

For permission to use material from this text or product, submit a request online at: www.thomsonrights.com

Any additional questions about permissions can be submitted by e-mail to: thomsonrights@thomson.com

Trademarks

Course ILT is a trademark of Course Technology.

Some of the product names and company names used in this book have been used for identification purposes only and may be trademarks or registered trademarks of their respective manufacturers and sellers.

Disclaimers

Course Technology reserves the right to revise this publication and make changes from time to time in its content without notice.

*The ProCert Labs numerical rating referenced is based on an independent review of this instructional material and is a separate analysis independent of Certiport or the Microsoft Office Specialist program.

Microsoft, the Office Logo, Excel, Outlook, and PowerPoint are either registered trademarks or trademarks of Microsoft Corporation in the United States and/or other countries. The Microsoft Office Specialist Logo is used under license from owner.

Certiport and the Certiport Approved Courseware logo are registered trademarks of Certiport Inc. in the United States and/or other countries.

Course Technology is independent from Microsoft Corporation or Certiport, and not affiliated with Microsoft or Certiport in any manner. While this publication may be used in assisting individuals to prepare for a Microsoft Office Specialist exam, Microsoft, Certiport, and Course Technology do not warrant that use of this publication will ensure passing a Microsoft Office Specialist exam.

1-4239-5938-8

Printed in the United States of America

1 2 3 4 5 WS 06 05 04 03

What does the Microsoft® Office Specialist Approved Courseware logo represent?

Only the finest courseware receives approval to bear the Microsoft® Office Specialist logo. In order to give candidates the greatest chance of success at becoming a Microsoft Office Specialist, all approved courseware has been reviewed by an independent third party for quality of content and adherence to exam objectives. This specific course has been mapped to the following Microsoft Office Specialist Exam Skill Standards:

- Access 2003 Specialist

What is Microsoft Office Specialist certification?

Microsoft Office Specialist certification shows that employees, candidates and students have something exceptional to offer—proven expertise in Microsoft Office programs. Recognized by businesses and schools around the world, it is the only Microsoft-approved certification program of its kind. There are four levels of certification available: Specialist, Expert, Master, and Master Instructor.[1] Certification is available for the following Microsoft Office programs:

- Microsoft Word
- Microsoft PowerPoint®
- Microsoft Excel®
- Microsoft Outlook®
- Microsoft Access
- Microsoft Project

For more information

To learn more about becoming a Microsoft Office Specialist, visit www.microsoft.com/officespecialist.

To learn about other Microsoft Office Specialist approved courseware from Course Technology, visit www.course.com.

---

[1]The availability of Microsoft Office Specialist certification exams varies by Microsoft Office program, program version, and language. Visit www.microsoft.com/officespecialist for exam availability.

Contents

Introduction   iii
    Topic A: About the manual iv
    Topic B: Setting your expectations viii
    Topic C: Re-keying the course xii

Getting started   1-1
    Topic A: Database concepts 1-2
    Topic B: Exploring the Access environment 1-4
    Topic C: Getting help 1-11
    Topic D: Closing a database and Access 1-14
    Unit summary: Getting started 1-16

Databases and tables   2-1
    Topic A: Planning and designing databases 2-2
    Topic B: Exploring tables 2-8
    Topic C: Creating tables 2-16
    Unit summary: Databases and tables 2-27

Fields and records   3-1
    Topic A: Changing the design of a table 3-2
    Topic B: Finding and editing records 3-7
    Topic C: Organizing records 3-12
    Unit summary: Fields and records 3-21

Data entry rules   4-1
    Topic A: Setting field properties 4-2
    Topic B: Working with input masks 4-9
    Topic C: Setting validation rules 4-14
    Topic D: Using indexes 4-18
    Unit summary: Data entry rules 4-20

Simple queries   5-1
    Topic A: Creating and using queries 5-2
    Topic B: Modifying query results and queries 5-12
    Topic C: Performing operations in queries 5-16
    Unit summary: Simple queries 5-26

Using forms   6-1
    Topic A: Creating forms 6-2
    Topic B: Using the Form Wizard 6-9
    Topic C: Using Design view 6-12
    Topic D: Finding, sorting, and filtering records 6-22
    Unit summary: Using forms 6-26

Working with reports   7-1
    Topic A: Creating reports 7-2
    Topic B: Modifying and printing reports 7-15
    Unit summary: Working with reports 7-29

Microsoft Office Specialist exam objectives map   A-1
    Topic A: Comprehensive exam objectives A-2

Course summary   S-1
    Topic A: Course summary S-2
    Topic B: Continued learning after class S-4

Quick reference   Q-1

Glossary   G-1

Index   I-1

Introduction

After reading this introduction, you will know how to:

A Use Course Technology ILT manuals in general.

B Use prerequisites, a target student description, course objectives, and a skills inventory to properly set your expectations for the course.

C Re-key this course after class.

Topic A: About the manual

Course Technology ILT philosophy

Course Technology ILT manuals facilitate your learning by providing structured interaction with the software itself. While we provide text to explain difficult concepts, the hands-on activities are the focus of our courses. By paying close attention as your instructor leads you through these activities, you will learn the skills and concepts effectively.

We believe strongly in the instructor-led classroom. During class, focus on your instructor. Our manuals are designed and written to facilitate your interaction with your instructor, and not to call attention to manuals themselves.

We believe in the basic approach of setting expectations, delivering instruction, and providing summary and review afterwards. For this reason, lessons begin with objectives and end with summaries. We also provide overall course objectives and a course summary to provide both an introduction to and closure on the entire course.

Manual components

The manuals contain these major components:

- Table of contents
- Introduction
- Units
- Appendix
- Course summary
- Quick reference
- Glossary
- Index

Each element is described below.

Table of contents

The table of contents acts as a learning roadmap.

Introduction

The introduction contains information about our training philosophy and our manual components, features, and conventions. It contains target student, prerequisite, objective, and setup information for the specific course.

Units

Units are the largest structural component of the course content. A unit begins with a title page that lists objectives for each major subdivision, or topic, within the unit. Within each topic, conceptual and explanatory information alternates with hands-on activities. Units conclude with a summary comprising one paragraph for each topic, and an independent practice activity that gives you an opportunity to practice the skills you've learned.

The conceptual information takes the form of text paragraphs, exhibits, lists, and tables. The activities are structured in two columns, one telling you what to do, the other providing explanations, descriptions, and graphics.

Appendix

The appendix for this course lists the Microsoft Office Specialist exam objectives for Microsoft Access 2003 along with references to corresponding coverage in Course ILT courseware.

Course summary

This section provides a text summary of the entire course. It is useful for providing closure at the end of the course. The course summary also indicates the next course in this series, if there is one, and lists additional resources you might find useful as you continue to learn about the software.

Quick reference

The quick reference is an at-a-glance job aid summarizing some of the more common features of the software.

Glossary

The glossary provides definitions for all of the key terms used in this course.

Index

The index at the end of this manual makes it easy for you to find information about a particular software component, feature, or concept.

Manual conventions

We've tried to keep the number of elements and the types of formatting to a minimum in the manuals. This aids in clarity and makes the manuals more classically elegant looking. But there are some conventions and icons you should know about.

Convention	Description
Italic text	In conceptual text, indicates a new term or feature.
Bold text	In unit summaries, indicates a key term or concept. In an independent practice activity, indicates an explicit item that you select, choose, or type.
`Code font`	Indicates code or syntax.
`Longer strings of ▶ code will look ▶ like this.`	In the hands-on activities, any code that's too long to fit on a single line is divided into segments by one or more continuation characters (▶). This code should be entered as a continuous string of text.
Select **bold item**	In the left column of hands-on activities, bold sans-serif text indicates an explicit item that you select, choose, or type.
Keycaps like ⏎ ENTER	Indicate a key on the keyboard you must press.

Hands-on activities

The hands-on activities are the most important parts of our manuals. They are divided into two primary columns. The "Here's how" column gives short instructions to you about what to do. The "Here's why" column provides explanations, graphics, and clarifications. Here's a sample:

Do it!

A-1: Creating a commission formula

Here's how	Here's why
1 Open Sales	This is an oversimplified sales compensation worksheet. It shows sales totals, commissions, and incentives for five sales reps.
2 Observe the contents of cell F4	F4 ▼ = =E4*C_Rate The commission rate formulas use the name "C_Rate" instead of a value for the commission rate.

For these activities, we have provided a collection of data files designed to help you learn each skill in a real-world business context. As you work through the activities, you will modify and update these files. Of course, you might make a mistake and, therefore, want to re-key the activity starting from scratch. To make it easy to start over, you will rename each data file at the end of the first activity in which the file is modified. Our convention for renaming files is to add the word "My" to the beginning of the file name. In the above activity, for example, a file called "Sales" is being used for the first time. At the end of this activity, you would save the file as "My sales," thus leaving the "Sales" file unchanged. If you make a mistake, you can start over using the original "Sales" file.

In some activities, however, it may not be practical to rename the data file. If you want to retry one of these activities, ask your instructor for a fresh copy of the original data file.

Topic B: Setting your expectations

Properly setting your expectations is essential to your success. This topic will help you do that by providing:

- Prerequisites for this course
- A description of the target student at whom the course is aimed
- A list of the objectives for the course
- A skills assessment for the course

Course prerequisites

Before taking this course, you should be familiar with personal computers and the use of a keyboard and a mouse. Furthermore, this course assumes that you've completed the following courses or have equivalent experience:

- *Windows 2000: Basic* or *Windows XP: Basic*

Target student

You should be comfortable using a personal computer and Microsoft Windows 2000. You will get the most out of this course if your goal is to become proficient using the features of Microsoft Access, including the Table Wizard, AutoForm, the Report Wizard, and filters.

Microsoft Office Specialist certification

This course is designed to help you pass the exam for Access 2003. For complete certification training, you should complete this course as well as:

- *Access 2003: Intermediate*
- *Access 2003: Advanced*

Course objectives

These overall course objectives will give you an idea about what to expect from the course. It is also possible that they will help you see that this course is not the right one for you. If you think you either lack the prerequisite knowledge or already know most of the subject matter to be covered, you should let your instructor know that you think you are misplaced in the class.

Note: In addition to the general objectives listed below, specific Microsoft Office Specialist exam objectives are listed at the beginning of each topic. For a complete mapping of exam objectives to Course ILT content, see Appendix A.

After completing this course, you will know how to:

- Organize data efficiently by using a database management system; start Access and open Access databases; and use the Help feature.
- Plan and create a database; use Datasheet view and Design view; and create tables and work in tables.
- Modify a table's design; use the Find feature and the spelling checker; and sort, filter, and delete records.
- Set field properties; create input masks; set validation rules; and create single- and multiple-field indexes.

- Create queries, and sort and filter the results; modify queries; and perform operations in queries.
- Create, modify, and work with forms; and use them to find, sort, and filter records.
- Create reports by using AutoReport, the Report Wizard, Design view, and queries; and modify and print reports.

Skills inventory

Use the following form to gauge your skill level entering the class. For each skill listed, rate your familiarity from 1 to 5, with five being the most familiar. *This is not a test.* Rather, it is intended to provide you with an idea of where you're starting from at the beginning of class. If you're wholly unfamiliar with all the skills, you might not be ready for the class. If you think you already understand all of the skills, you might need to move on to the next course in the series. In either case, you should let your instructor know as soon as possible.

Skill	1	2	3	4	5
Identifying database components					
Starting and examining Access					
Opening a database					
Examining the Database window and a database table					
Using the Type a question for help box and the Office Assistant					
Closing a database and Access					
Planning and creating a database					
Examining a table in Datasheet view and Design view					
Creating a table by using the Table Wizard and Design view					
Adding fields to a table, and setting the primary key					
Saving and adding records					
Modifying field names, and deleting and inserting fields					
Finding and replacing values in a table					
Sorting records					
Filtering records					
Setting field properties					
Creating an input mask					
Creating indexes					
Creating queries by using the Simple Query Wizard and Design view					

Skill	1	2	3	4	5
Sorting and filtering query results					
Adding fields to and removing fields from a query					
Using comparison operators and calculations in a query					
Creating and modifying forms					
Finding, sorting, and filtering records in a form					
Creating reports					
Grouping and summarizing data in a report					
Printing a report					

Topic C: Re-keying the course

If you have the proper hardware and software, you can re-key this course after class. This section explains what you'll need in order to do so, and how to do it.

Computer requirements

For you to re-key this course, your personal computer must have:

- A keyboard and a mouse
- Pentium 233 MHz processor (or higher)
- At least 128 MB RAM
- 400 MB of available hard drive space
- CD-ROM drive
- SVGA or higher resolution monitor
- A printer driver (An actual printer is not required, but the printing activities will not work as described unless a printer driver is installed.)
- Internet access, if you want to download the Student Data files from www.courseilt.com, and for downloading the latest updates from www.windowsupdate.com

Setup instructions to re-key the course

Before you re-key the course, you will need to perform the following steps.

1 Install Microsoft Windows 2000 Professional on an NTFS partition according to the software manufacturer's instructions. Then, install the latest critical updates and service packs from www.windowsupdate.com. (You can also use Windows XP Professional, although the screen shots in this course were taken using Windows 2000, so your screens might look somewhat different.)

2 Adjust your computer's display properties as follows:
   a Open the Control Panel and double-click Display to open the Display Properties dialog box.
   b On the Settings tab, change the Colors setting to True Color (24 bit) and the Screen area to 800 by 600 pixels.
   c On the Appearance tab, set the Scheme to Windows Classic.
   d Click OK. If you are prompted to accept the new settings, click OK and click Yes. Then, if necessary, close the Display Properties dialog box.

3 Adjust your computer's Internet settings as follows:
   a On the desktop, right-click the Internet Explorer icon and choose Properties to open the Internet Properties dialog box.
   b On the Connections tab, click Setup to start the Internet Connection Wizard.
   c Click Cancel. A message box will appear.
   d Check "Do not show the Internet Connection wizard in the future," and then click Yes.
   e Re-open the Internet Properties dialog box.
   f On the General tab, click Use Blank, click Apply, and click OK.

4. Install Microsoft Office 2003 according to the software manufacturer's instructions as follows:
   a. When prompted for the CD key, enter the 25-character code included with your software.
   b. Select the Custom installation option and click Next.
   c. Clear all check boxes except Microsoft Access.
   d. Select "Choose advanced customization of applications" and click Next.
   e. Next to Microsoft Access for Windows, click the drop-down arrow and choose Run all from My Computer.
   f. Next to Office Shared Features, click the drop-down arrow and choose Run all from My Computer.
   g. Click Next. Then, click Install to start the installation.
   h. When the installation has completed successfully, click Finish.
5. Start Access. Then, turn off the Office Assistant as follows:
   a. If the Office Assistant is not displayed, choose Help, Show the Office Assistant.
   b. Right-click the Office Assistant and choose Options to open the Office Assistant dialog box.
   c. Clear Use the Office Assistant and click OK.
6. To ensure that you won't get a macro warning when they open tables in Access, do this:
   a. Choose Tools, Macro, Security.
   b. Select the Low security setting.
   c. Click OK.
7. Configure Access to always show full menus. Here's how:
   a. Choose View, Toolbars, Customize to open the Customize dialog box.
   b. On the Options tab, check Always show full menus.
   c. Click Close.
8. Close Access.
9. Disable the language bar:
   a. In the Control Panel, double-click Text Services to open the Text Services dialog box.
   b. Under Preferences, click Language Bar to open the Language Bar Settings dialog box.
   c. Clear Show the Language bar on the desktop, and then click OK.
   d. Click OK to close the Text Services dialog box.
   e. Close the control panel.
10. If necessary, install a printer driver. If a printer was connected to the computer during the installation of Windows, there will be a driver installed for that printer. If not, you should install a standard PostScript printer driver, such as the HP LaserJet 5.
11. Create a folder named Student Data at the root of the hard drive.

12 If necessary, download the Student Data files for the course. (If you don't have an Internet connection, you can ask your instructor for a copy of the data files on a disk.)

    a Connect to www.courseilt.com/instructor_tools.html.

    b Click the link for Microsoft Access 2003 to display a page of course listings, and then click the link for Access 2003: Basic, Second Edition.

    c Click the link for downloading the Student Data files, and follow the instructions that appear on your screen.

13 Copy the data files to the Student Data folder.

CertBlaster test preparation for Microsoft Office Specialist certification

If you are interested in attaining Microsoft Office Specialist certification, you can download CertBlaster test preparation software for Access 2003 from the Course ILT Web site. Here's what you do:

1 Go to www.courseilt.com/certblaster.
2 Click the link for Access 2003.
3 Save the .EXE file to a folder on your hard drive. (**Note**: If you skip this step, the CertBlaster software will not install correctly.)
4 Click Start and choose Run.
5 Click Browse and then navigate to the folder that contains the .EXE file.
6 Select the .EXE file and click Open.
7 Click OK and follow the on-screen instructions. When prompted for the password, enter **c_access**.

Unit 1
Getting started

Unit time: 30 minutes

Complete this unit, and you'll know how to:

A Organize data efficiently by using a database management system.

B Start Access, learn about its environment, open a database, and learn about database objects.

C Use Help options to get information on Access topics.

D Close a database, and close Access.

Topic A: Database concepts

Explanation

Microsoft Access, a component of the Microsoft Office suite, helps you store, organize, and retrieve information efficiently. Access is a database management system. A *database* is a collection of data, or information. An example of a simple database is a phone book that contains the names, phone numbers, and addresses of individuals and businesses. A *database management system (DBMS)* is a set of programs used to store and organize data and to make data retrieval efficient.

Database components

To become familiar with Access, you need to understand the basic database concepts. The following table defines several database-related terms:

Term	Description
Data value	An item of data. In Exhibit 1-1, 2 oz is a data value.
Record	A single set of related data values. In Exhibit 1-1, each row is a record because a row contains data for a single product.
Field	A specific type of information or data value in a table. In Exhibit 1-1, each column represents a field. Field 1 contains the product IDs, and Field 2 contains the product names.
Table	A collection of records. The records and fields in a table form its rows and columns. Exhibit 1-1 shows a table named tblProduct. It contains four fields and ten records.

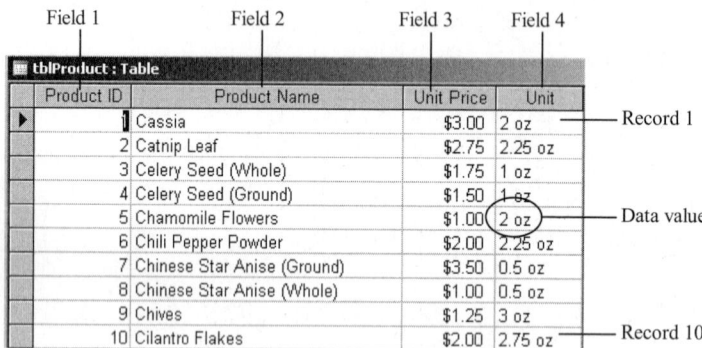

Exhibit 1-1: The tblProduct table

Getting started **1–3**

Do it!

A-1: Identifying database components

Here's how	Here's why
1 Observe the table	As shown in Exhibit 1-1. This table contains ten rows and four columns.
2 Observe the column headings	The headings are Product ID, Product Name, Unit Price, and Unit. Each column represents a field.
3 Observe the data values in each field	Each field contains a specific type of data value.
4 Observe the rows	Each row contains data for a single product. For example, the fifth row contains data about chamomile flowers.

Relational databases

Explanation

Microsoft Access is an RDBMS. A *relational database management system (RDBMS)* is a type of DBMS in which data is organized in the form of related tables. In related tables, one or more fields are linked to fields in another table. This link ensures that you can enter only those values that have corresponding entries in the other table. For example, suppose that you store product details and sales details in two tables. These tables can be related by using the common field Productid. This ensures that you cannot enter the sales details of any products that are not available in the product details table.

Any database that uses an RDBMS to organize data is known as a *relational database*. This database can have multiple tables that contain data about various entities, such as products, sales, or customers. An *entity* is any object that has a distinct set of properties. A relational database helps you store data in an orderly manner so that you can retrieve it efficiently. For example, if you need to display the product details and sales details in a single report, you can access the corresponding tables to get the information.

Do it!

A-2: Identifying the advantages of relational databases

Questions and answers
1 What is a relational database?
2 Microsoft Access is an RDBMS. True or false?
3 What are the advantages of using a relational database?

Topic B: Exploring the Access environment

Explanation

You start Access by choosing Start, Programs, Microsoft Office, Microsoft Office Access 2003. The Access window contains components such as a menu bar, a title bar, and a status bar. After opening the Access window, you can create databases and tables.

Components of the Access window

The following table describes the Access window components, shown in Exhibit 1-2:

Component	Description
Menu bar	The menu bar shows all the menus available in Access. A *menu* contains commands to perform a set of related tasks. For example, the File menu contains commands to perform file management tasks, such as opening, saving, printing, or closing a file.
Title bar	The title bar contains buttons you can use to change the window size or close the window. The title bar also displays the Control menu icon and the program name. The Control menu icon, on the extreme left side of the title bar, opens a menu that contains commands for minimizing, maximizing, and closing the window.
Database toolbar	The Database toolbar contains buttons for frequently used actions, such as opening or saving a file. These buttons are shortcuts to some of the available commands in the menus.
Task pane	The task pane contains shortcuts to frequently performed tasks. For example, you can use the Getting Started task pane to create or open a database, use the Clipboard task pane to view the contents of the Clipboard, and use the Basic File Search task pane to search for a file.
Status bar	The status bar displays the current status of ongoing tasks. It displays "Ready" when a database is opened, and displays information about the fields when a table is opened.

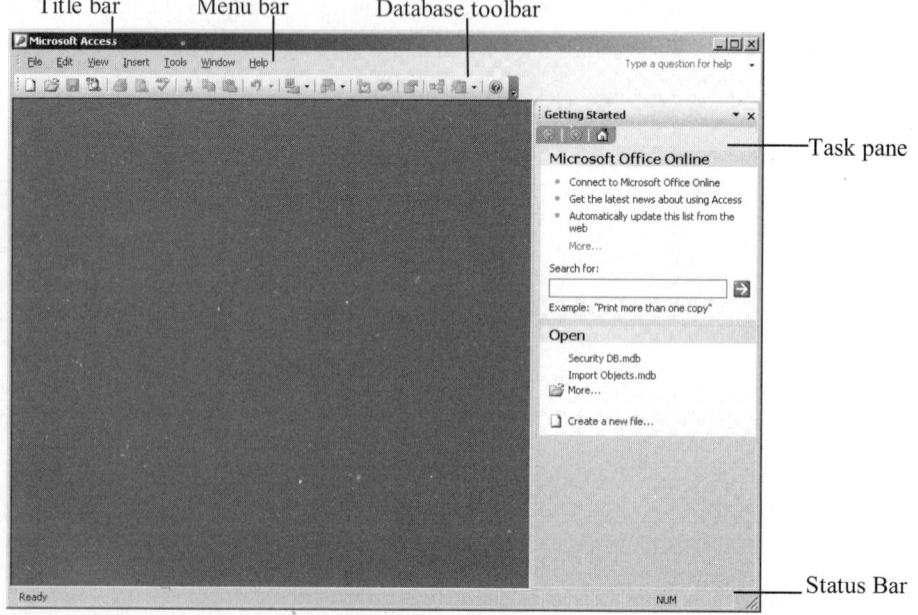

Exhibit 1-2: The components of the Access window

Getting started **1–5**

Do it!

B-1: Starting Access and examining the Access window

Here's how	Here's why
1 Choose **Start**, **Programs**, **Microsoft Office**, **Microsoft Office Access 2003**	(To start Access.) The Microsoft Access window appears, as shown in Exhibit 1-2.
2 Observe the title bar	The title bar contains the Control menu icon, the title Microsoft Office Access, and the buttons to minimize, restore, and close the window.
3 Observe the menu bar	The menu bar includes the commands File, Edit, View, Insert, Tools, Window, and Help.
4 Choose **View**	
	(Point to View and click.) The View menu commands include Database Objects, List, Details, Properties, Code, Toolbars, and Refresh. These commands control how you view the Access window.
Click anywhere on the screen	To close the View menu.
5 Observe the task pane	The Getting Started task pane appears by default. You use this pane to open and create databases. You can show or hide the task pane by choosing View, Toolbars, Task Pane.

Opening databases

Explanation

To open a database, you use the Open dialog box. You can open this dialog box in any of these ways:

- Choose File, Open.
- In the Getting Started task pane, click Open under the Open section.
- On the Database toolbar, click the Open button.

In the Open dialog box, specify the name of the folder and database you want to open, and then click the Open button. You can also click the file name under the Open section in the Getting Started task pane.

When you open or create a database, its file format appears in the Database window along with its name. The *file format* is the specific format in which each application stores data. By default, Access 2003 creates databases in the Access 2000 file format. As a result, a database you create in Access 2003 can be opened in Access 2000 as well.

Do it!

B-2: Opening a database

Here's how	Here's why
1 Choose **File, Open...**	The Open dialog box appears.
2 Navigate to the current unit folder within the Student Data folder	To display the files in the current unit folder.
Select **Concepts**	(If necessary.) You'll open this database.
Click **Open**	
3 Observe the title of the Database window	The title bar displays "Concepts : Database (Access 2000 file format)." Access 2003 uses the Access 2000 file format for its databases.

Exploring the Database window

Explanation

The Database window contains the title bar, the toolbar, and the Objects bar.

- The title bar shows the name of the active database.
- The Objects bar (in the left pane of the Database window) shows various database elements, or objects, such as tables, forms, and queries. Each button on the Objects bar refers to a specific type of object, as shown in Exhibit 1-3. When you click an object button, you'll see various options to create that object and you'll see the names of the existing objects of that type in the right pane. For example, if you click the Tables button on the Objects bar, you'll see the list of options for creating tables and a list of available tables, if any.
- The toolbar (at the top of the Database window) contains buttons such as Open and New, which you can use to open existing objects and create objects, respectively.

Exhibit 1-3: The Database window

Access database objects

The following table describes the objects in an Access database:

Object	Description
Table	Used to store data. For example, you can use a table to store details about employees, such as name, title, and department.
Query	Used to retrieve specific information—such as which product had the highest sales for a given month—from a table.
Form	Used to enter data into a table in a database. You can also use a form to view and modify records in a table.
Report	Used for presenting data in a printed format. You can customize a report by applying different font styles and headings.
Page	Used to show table data on the Internet.
Macro	Used to automate frequently performed database tasks, such as printing a set of weekly reports.
Module	Used to automate and customize database operations. Modules are programs written in Visual Basic.
Group	Used to organize database objects through shortcuts.

Getting started **1–9**

Do it!

B-3: Examining the Database window

Here's how	Here's why
1 Observe the buttons on the Database window toolbar	(As shown in Exhibit 1-3.) The Database window toolbar contains buttons such as Open, Design, and New. You use these buttons to open or modify objects and to create new objects.
2 Observe the Objects bar	*[Objects bar showing: Tables, Queries, Forms, Reports, Pages, Macros, Modules; Groups: Favorites]* You can switch between the types of database objects—such as tables, queries, forms, and reports—by clicking the buttons on the Objects bar. When you click an object button, Access displays options for creating that object and displays the names of existing objects of that type.
3 On the Objects bar, click **Tables**	(If necessary.) To see the list of table objects.
4 Observe the list	*[List showing: Create table in Design view, Create table by using wizard, Create table by entering data, tblOrder, tblOrderItem, tblProduct, tblRetailer]* It shows that there are four tables in this database and contains options to create a table in Design view, by using the wizard, and by entering data.
5 Click **Queries**	(The Queries button is on the Objects bar.) To see the list of query objects. The name of the existing query object is qryProduct. The list also contains options for creating queries.

Open a database table

Explanation

You need to open a table to examine its contents. To open a table, click Tables on the Objects bar. Select the name of the table object you want to open, and click the Open button. You can also right-click the name of the table and choose Open from the shortcut menu, or you can simply double-click the table name.

Do it!

B-4: Examining a database table

Here's how	Here's why
1 In the Objects bar, click **Tables**	You'll open a table.
2 In the right pane, select **tblProduct**	You'll view the contents of this table.
Click **Open**	(The Open button is on the Database window toolbar.) To open the tblProduct table. There are 24 rows in this table.
3 Observe the headings in the Table window	The table has four fields. The field headings are Product ID, Product Name, Unit Price, and Unit.
4 Observe the rows and columns in the table	Each row corresponds to a record, and each column corresponds to a field.
5 Choose **File**, **Close**	To close the table.

Topic C: Getting help

Explanation

The Help menu is in the menu bar of the Access window. When you choose Microsoft Access Help from the Help menu or press F1, the Microsoft Access Help task pane appears, as shown in Exhibit 1-4. In the Search field, under Assistance, enter the topic you want to search for.

There are different ways to access Help:
- Choose Help, Microsoft Access Help.
- Press F1.
- Click the Microsoft Access Help button on the toolbar.
- Use the "Type a question for help" box.
- Use the Office Assistant.

Exhibit 1-4: The Microsoft Access Help task pane

Type a question for help box

You can search for information by using the Type a question for help box, which is on the left of the menu bar, as shown in Exhibit 1-5. You type a question or a keyword in the box and press Enter. A list of corresponding help topics appears. Select the relevant topic from the list to view the detailed information in the Microsoft Help window.

Exhibit 1-5: The menu bar with the Type a question for help box

1–12 Access 2003: Basic

Do it!

C-1: Using the Type a question for help box

Here's how	Here's why
1 In the Type a question for help box, enter **database**	You'll search for information related to the term "database."
2 Press [← ENTER]	
	Search Results pane showing 30 results from Office Online: Introduction to databases (Training > Access), Table that data (Training > Access), Create an Access database (Help > Creating and Working with Databases and Objects), Open an Access database (Help > Working with Access Files), Ways to get started if you're using a database for the first time (Help > Startup and Settings), Ways to get started if you've used other databases...
	A list of related topics appears in the Search Results task pane.
3 Click **About Access databases**	The Microsoft Office Access Help window appears. The window displays help on the selected topic.
Click **Show All**	(At the top of the Microsoft Office Access Help window.) To view the help text of all the subtopics displayed in the Help window. You'll need to scroll down to view all the text.
Click **Hide All**	(At the top of the Microsoft Office Access Help window.) To collapse all the subtopics.
4 Close the Microsoft Access Help window	In the Microsoft Office Access Help window, click the close button.

Office Assistant

Explanation

The Office Assistant is an animated character that helps you interact with the Access Help feature. You can use the Office Assistant to get specific information about Access. The default character for the animated object is a paper clip.

To use the Office Assistant:

1. Choose Help, Show the Office Assistant.
2. Click the Office Assistant to display the "What would you like to do?" balloon.
3. In the box, enter the text you want to search for, and click Search.

Do it!

C-2: Using the Office Assistant

Here's how	Here's why
1 Choose **Help**, **Show the Office Assistant**	The Office Assistant appears.
2 Click the **Office Assistant**	(If necessary.) To display the "What would you like to do?" balloon.
3 In the box, enter **What is a table?**	You'll search for information related to tables.
4 Click **Search**	To display the help topics. A list of topics related to the question in the "What would you like to do?" balloon appears in the Search Results task pane. Click a topic to get information about that topic.
Click **About tables**	Two subtopics appear.
Click **About tables (MDB)**	Help on this topic appears in the Microsoft Office Access Help window.
Close the Help window	
5 Choose **Help**, **Hide the Office Assistant**	To hide the Office Assistant.

Topic D: Closing a database and Access

Explanation

When you've finished working with a database, you need to close the database and then close Microsoft Access.

Closing a database

There are several ways to close an Access database. These are:

- Choose File, Close.
- Click the Close button in the Database window.
- Double-click the Database Control menu icon in the Database window.
- Click the Database Control menu icon in the Database window, and choose Close.

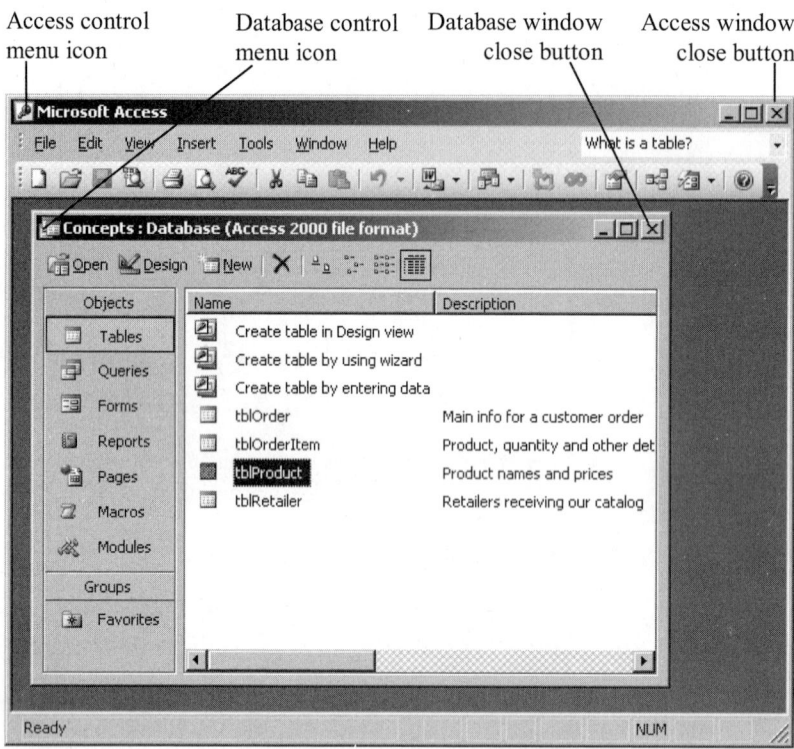

Exhibit 1-6: The Control menu icons and the Close buttons

Closing Access

There are several ways to close Access:
- Choose File, Exit.
- Double-click the Access Control menu icon, which is on the extreme left of the title bar.
- Click the Access Control menu icon to display the Control menu, and then choose Close.
- Press Alt+F4.
- Click the Close button in the Access window.

Do it!

D-1: Closing a database and Access

Here's how	Here's why
1 Choose **File**, **Close**	To close the database.
2 Choose **File**, **Exit**	To close Access.

Unit summary: Getting started

Topic A In this topic, you learned that a **database** is used to store data in the form of **tables**. You learned that a table contains **records** and **fields**. You also learned about **relational databases**, which store data in related tables.

Topic B In this topic, you learned how to start Access and you examined the **Microsoft Access** window. You learned about the menu bar, the title bar, the Database toolbar, and the status bar. You also opened a database, examined the **Database window**, and learned how to open a **table**.

Topic C In this topic, you learned how to use the **Help** feature. You learned how to get information on various Access topics by using the Help menu and the Help toolbar button. You also learned how to get help by using the **Type a question for help** box and the **Office Assistant**.

Topic D In this topic, you learned how to **close a database** and **close Access**.

Independent practice activity

1. Start Access.
2. In the Access window, identify the toolbar, the menu bar, and the title bar.
3. Open PracticeConcepts (from the current unit folder).
4. Identify the types and number of database objects in the database. (*Hint:* Click the different database object buttons in the Objects bar.)
5. Open the tblEmployee table. How many fields and records are there in this table?
6. Close the tblEmployee table.
7. Close the PracticeConcepts database.
8. Close Access.

Review questions

1. Identify the correct term for each of the following:

Description	Term
A set of related data values	
A collection of records	
An item of data	

2 Let's say you're working with a database that contains information about the salespeople at Outlander Spices. Which object you would use in each of the following situations?

Situation	Object
You want to enter information for a new salesperson.	
You want to know which departments have earnings of more than $80,000.	
You want to print all the values from the table.	

3 What is a relational database?

4 Name two ways to access the Help system.

5 What is the Office Assistant?

Unit 2
Databases and tables

Unit time: 60 minutes

Complete this unit, and you'll know how to:

A Plan and create a database.

B Examine a table in Datasheet view and Design view.

C Create and modify tables.

Topic A: Planning and designing databases

This topic covers the following Microsoft Office Specialist exam objectives.

#	Objective
AC03S-1-1	Creating databases using Database Wizard
AC03S-1-1	Creating blank databases

Planning databases

Explanation

Before you create a database, it's important that you plan the type of data you need to store. For example, if you're keeping track of a company's products, sales, and retailers, you must plan and design a database that can store the data related to all products, sales, and retailers. This data should be stored in three separate tables so you can distinguish between these three sets of information. You'll also need to plan how you'll be using the information stored in the database. Thorough planning ensures that no data is missing or redundant, and it saves time on future modifications to the database.

To plan a database, you must determine:

- The purpose of the database
- The number of tables and the type of information you'll store in each table
- The fields that will be used in each table
- The types of queries you'll want to perform on the database
- The forms you'll need to create
- The types of reports you'll need to generate

Do it!

A-1: Planning a database

Questions and answers

1 You work in the Sales and Marketing department of Outlander Spices. You keep track of the company's retailers, and you want to create a database of information related to the operations in your department. What is the purpose of the database?

2 While creating the database, how many tables will you need to create, and what type of information do you need to store in each table?

3 Identify some of the fields that you'll need to create in the tables.

4 What kind of information could you to extract from these tables by using queries?

Creating a database

Explanation

After you've planned and designed a database, you're ready to create it. You can create a database either by using the Database Wizard or by starting with a blank database.

Rules for naming databases and objects

When naming a database or any database object, you should keep in mind several naming rules. These include the following:

- The name can contain letters, numbers, special characters, and embedded spaces.
- The name cannot contain more than 64 characters.
- The name cannot start with a space.

It's a good practice to use an underscore (_) instead of an embedded space in a database name or an object name. However, database object names cannot include a period (.), an exclamation mark (!), an accent grave (`), or brackets ([]).

The Database Wizard

You can use the Database Wizard to automatically create databases and database objects. You can also specify a database structure from the ten types of database structures that Access provides. These database structures are called *templates*. Based on the template you select, the Database Wizard will create the database and database objects for you.

To create a database by using the Database Wizard:

1. Choose File, New, or click the New button on the Database toolbar. The New File task pane appears.
2. In the task pane, under the Templates section, click On my computer to open the Templates dialog box.
3. Click the Databases tab. From the list of database templates, select the relevant template.
4. Click OK to open the File New Database dialog box.
5. From the Save in list, select the location where you want to save the database.
6. In the File name box, enter the name of the database. Click Create to open the Database Wizard.
7. Follow the steps in the wizard, and click Finish.

Databases and tables **2–5**

Do it! **A-2: Using the Database Wizard**

Here's how	Here's why
1 Start Access	Choose Start, Programs, Microsoft Office, Microsoft Office Access 2003.
2 Choose **File**, **New…**	(If necessary.) To display the New File task pane.
3 Under Templates, click **On my computer…**	**Templates** Search online for: [ ] [Go] Templates on Office Online On my computer… (In the New File task pane.) To open the Templates dialog box. By default, the General tab is activated.
4 Click the **Databases** tab	To see the different database templates available.
5 Select **Order Entry**	You'll create a database for maintaining details about the company, employees, products, orders, and other transactions.
Click **OK**	To open the File New Database dialog box.
6 In the Save in list, navigate to the current unit folder	You'll save the database in this folder.
Edit the File name box to read **Outlander_Spices**	To specify the name of the new database.
Click **Create**	The Database Wizard dialog box appears. It displays the details that you'll store in this database.
7 Click **Next**	(To move to the next step of the Database Wizard.) You'll see the lists of tables and fields in the tables.
8 Click **Next**	You'll see the list of various styles for creating forms. By default, Standard style is selected.
9 Click **Next**	You'll see the list of various styles for creating reports. By default, Corporate is selected.
10 Click **Next**	
Edit the What would you like the title of the database to be box to read **Outlander Spices**	To specify the title for the database.

11	Click **Next**	
	Verify that Yes, start the database is checked	To open the database after you exit the wizard.
12	Click **Finish**	A dialog box with a progress bar first appears, indicating the rate at which the database objects are being created. Then, a message box appears prompting you to enter details about the company.
	Click **OK**	To open the My Company Information form.
13	Enter the details as shown	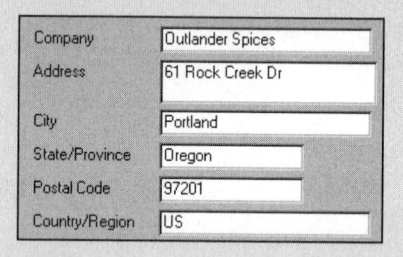 Company: Outlander Spices Address: 61 Rock Creek Dr City: Portland State/Province: Oregon Postal Code: 97201 Country/Region: US
	Close the window	The Main Switchboard form appears with options for you to use the database.
14	Click as shown	(Restore Up button on Outlander Spices form)
		(The Outlander Spices Database window is in the lower-left corner of the Access window.) To restore the window. You'll view the forms created with the Database Wizard.
	Observe the Outlander Spices Database window	It shows the forms created by the Database Wizard.
	On the Objects bar, click **Tables**	To view the tables created by the Database Wizard. Ten tables were created.
	On the Objects bar, click **Reports**	To view the reports created by the Database Wizard. Six reports were created.
15	Click the Main Switchboard form	(The Main Switchboard form is behind the Outlander Spices Database window.) To bring the form forward. You'll close the database.
16	Click as shown	(Exit this database button)
		To close the database.

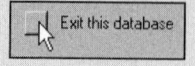

Creating blank databases

Explanation

When you create a blank database, you'll initially see only the Database window. You must then manually create the objects you want to include in the database. This manual method is more flexible because you can create custom tables and fields, instead of using a predefined design provided by the Database Wizard.

To create a blank Access database:

1 Open the New File task pane. Under the New section, click Blank database.
2 In the File New Database dialog box, specify the location and the name of the database.
3 Click Create.

Do it!

A-3: Creating a blank database

Here's how	Here's why
1 Click	(The New button is on the Database toolbar.) To display the New File task pane.
2 In the task pane, under New, click **Blank database...**	To open the File New Database dialog box. You'll specify the name and location of the new database here.
3 Navigate to the current unit folder	(If necessary.) You'll save the database in this folder.
4 Edit the File name box to read **CreateDatabase**	To specify the name of the new database.
Click **Create**	(To create the database.) The task pane closes the CreateDatabase : Database (Access 2000 file format) window appears.
5 Choose **File**, **Close**	To close the database.

Topic B: Exploring tables

This topic covers the following Microsoft Office Specialist exam objectives.

#	Objective
AC03S-2-1	Entering records into a datasheet (This objective is also covered in Topic C.)
AC03S-2-2	Using navigation controls to move among records
AC03S-4-2	Using datasheet, Pivot Chart, Web page, and layout views
	This objective is also covered in:
	• Topic C of this unit
	• The unit titled "Working with reports"
	• *Access 2003: Intermediate*, in the units titled "Internet integration" and "PivotTables and PivotCharts")

Views

Explanation

For working with databases, Access provides several views, such as Datasheet, Design, Pivot Table, and Pivot Chart.

Datasheet view displays data in a tabular format, containing rows and columns. Datasheet view helps you scroll through records and add, edit, or view data in a table.

If you want to change the design of a table by adding or changing field details, you can do it in Design view. *Design view* gives you complete control over the table's structure.

To switch between Datasheet view and Design view, use the View button on the Table Datasheet or Table Design toolbars, respectively.

Pivot Table view helps you analyze data. *Pivot Chart* view helps you display data graphically in Datasheet view.

Do it!

B-1: Discussing views

Questions and answers

1 When you want to add or edit data in a table, which view will you work with?

2 If you want to modify the structure of a table, which view will you use?

3 Which view will help you in analyzing data?

4 You want to present the analysis of sales data in a meeting. Which view will you use?

Datasheet view

Explanation

When you open a table, it opens in Datasheet view, as shown in Exhibit 2-1. Each column in Datasheet view is a field, and each row is a record. Use the navigation buttons and scrollbars to scroll through the table. You can scroll to the left or to the right of the window by using the horizontal scrollbar. You can scroll up and down by using the vertical scrollbar.

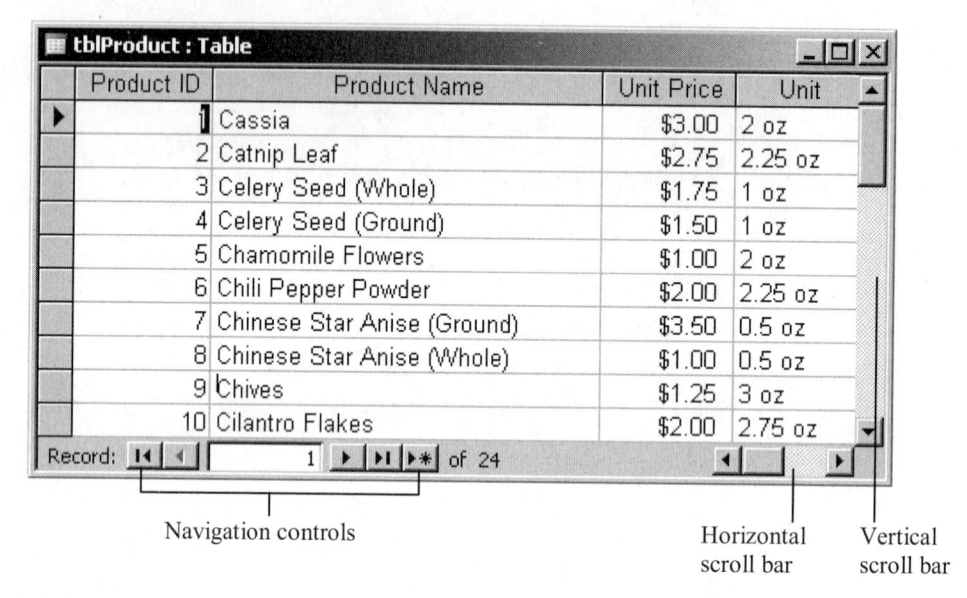

Product ID	Product Name	Unit Price	Unit
1	Cassia	$3.00	2 oz
2	Catnip Leaf	$2.75	2.25 oz
3	Celery Seed (Whole)	$1.75	1 oz
4	Celery Seed (Ground)	$1.50	1 oz
5	Chamomile Flowers	$1.00	2 oz
6	Chili Pepper Powder	$2.00	2.25 oz
7	Chinese Star Anise (Ground)	$3.50	0.5 oz
8	Chinese Star Anise (Whole)	$1.00	0.5 oz
9	Chives	$1.25	3 oz
10	Cilantro Flakes	$2.00	2.75 oz

Exhibit 2-1: The tblProduct table in Datasheet view

Do it!

B-2: Examining a table in Datasheet view

Here's how	Here's why
1 Choose **File**, **Open...**	To display the Open dialog box.
Select **AccessBasics**	(If necessary.)
Click **Open**	To open the database. The AccessBasics : Database (Access 2000 file format) window appears.
2 On the Objects bar, click **Tables**	(If necessary.) To view the list of tables in the database. There are four tables: tblOrder, tblOrderItem, tblProduct, and tblRetailer.
Select **tblProduct**	You'll examine this table.
Click **Open**	(To open the tblProduct : Table window, shown in Exhibit 2-1.) The tblProduct table is shown in Datasheet view.
3 Observe the fields in the table	Each column in the table represents a field. The fields are Product ID, Product Name, Unit Price, and Unit.
Observe the records in the table	Each row in the table represents a record. There are 24 records in the table. You can add, edit, or delete records in Datasheet view.
Observe the lower-left area of the Datasheet window	In this area, "1 of 24" appears, indicating that the first record is now active and that there are 24 records in the table.

Navigating in a table

Explanation

In Datasheet view, you can navigate in a table by using the navigation buttons, as shown in Exhibit 2-2. These are located at the bottom of the Datasheet view window.

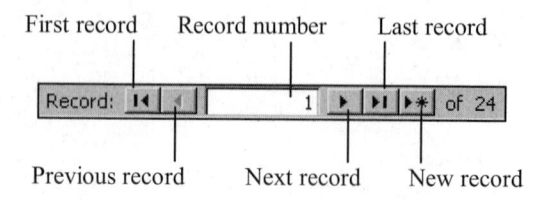

Exhibit 2-2: The navigation buttons and the record number box in Datasheet view

Using the record selector

You can also navigate through the records and select specific records by using the *record selector*, which points to the currently active record and indicates its status. The record selector is the small box to the left of each record in a table. If you click in this box, the record next to it is highlighted, making it the active record. The icon for the record selector changes based on the status of the record. The following table explains the different icons for the record selector:

Icon	Description
▶	Indicates the current or active record.
✎	Indicates that you are in the process of editing the record but have not yet saved it.
✱	Indicates that you can enter data for a new record.

Do it!

B-3: Navigating in a table in Datasheet view

Here's how	Here's why
1 Verify that the tblProduct table is open in Datasheet view	Product ID / Product Name — 1 Cassia, 2 Catnip Leaf. The record selector is on the left side of the data value 1.
2 Observe the record number box	1 (At the bottom of the Datasheet view window.) It indicates that record 1 is the active record.
Click ▶	(The next record button is at the bottom of the Datasheet window.) To move to the next record. The record selector moves to the left side of 2.
Observe the record number box	The record number box contains the value 2.

Databases and tables   **2–13**

3	Click ◄	(To move to the previous record.) The record selector is positioned to the left of the first row.
4	Click ►❙	(To move to the last record.) The record selector is now next to the twenty-fourth record.
5	Click ❙◄	(To move to the first record.) The record number 1 is shown in the record number box.
	Edit the record number box to read **5**	You'll move to the fifth record.
	Press (← ENTER)	The record selector is next to the fifth record.
6	Click ►✱	To add a new record.
7	In the Product Name field of the new record, enter **Ancho Pepper (Ground)**	The value in the Product ID field automatically changes to 35. This occurs because the Product ID field is set to a numeric data type that will automatically increment by one each time you add a record.
	Observe the record selector	It takes the shape of a pencil indicating that you are in the process of editing a record.
	Press (TAB)	To move to the next cell.
8	In the Unit Price field, enter **12.75**	
	Press (TAB)	To move to the next cell.
	In the Unit field, enter **2 oz**	
9	Press (TAB)	(To move to the next record.) The new record is saved automatically when you move to a different record or close the table.

Design view

Explanation

The design of a table consists of the field names, the type of data each field stores, the field size, and the manner in which field values will appear in the table. When you want to specify the properties of a field, such as Field Name and Data Type, you create a table in Design view. In this view, the window is split into two horizontal panes, as shown in Exhibit 2-3.

The upper pane displays the design of the table in the following terms:

- **Field Name** — The name of each field.
- **Data Type** — The type of data stored in each field. For example, the Text data type stores text values, and Number data type stores numbers.
- **Description** — Explanation of the field's purpose.

The lower pane is the Field Properties pane. Here, you can see the properties, or attributes, of each field, including Field Size, Format, and Caption. The Format property specifies the way the data should appear in the table. The Caption property helps you specify titles for fields. These captions appear as field headings in the Datasheet view of the table. If you don't specify captions for the fields, the field names appear as the field headings. The other field properties vary depending on the data type of the field.

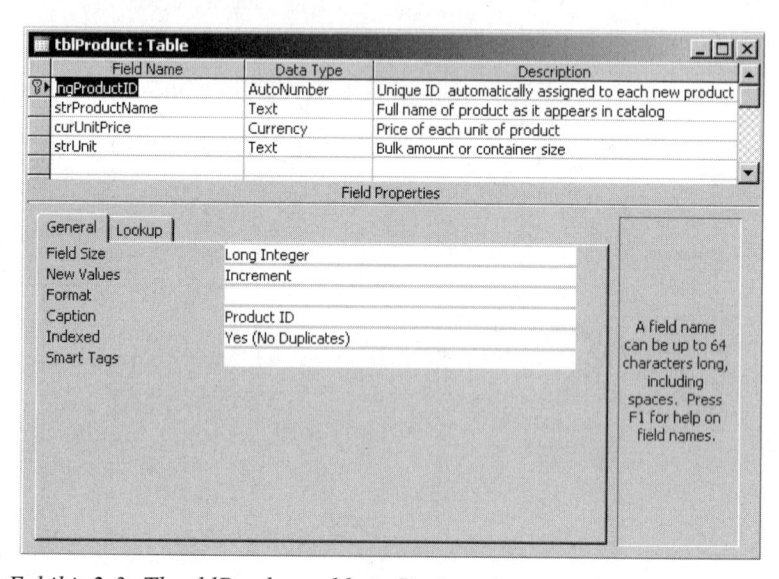

Exhibit 2-3: The tblProduct table in Design view

Databases and tables **2–15**

Do it! **B-4: Examining a table in Design view**

Here's how	Here's why
1 Click [icon]	(The View button is on the Table Datasheet toolbar.) To switch to Design view.
2 Observe the window	The tblProduct : Table window appears in Design view, as shown in Exhibit 2-3.
3 Observe the Field Name column	The Field Name column lists the fields in the table. The fields are lngProduct ID, strProductName, curUnitPrice, and strUnit. The corresponding field headings in Datasheet view are Product ID, Product Name, Unit Price, and Unit.
4 Observe the Data Type column	The data type for lngProductID is AutoNumber; the data type for strProductName and strUnit is Text; and the data type for curUnitPrice is Currency.
5 Observe the Description column	Each field has a description.
6 Observe the Field Properties pane	This pane shows the field properties specific to different data types. Exhibit 2-3 shows the properties of the lngProductID field.
7 Choose **File**, **Close**	To close Design view.
8 Close the database	Choose File, Close.

Topic C: Creating tables

This topic covers the following Microsoft Office Specialist exam objectives.

#	Objective
AC03S-1-2	Creating tables using Table Wizard
AC03S-1-2	Modifying table properties or structure (This objective is also covered in the unit titled "Fields and records.")
AC03S-1-3	Changing field types (This objective is also covered in the unit titled "Fields and records.")
AC03S-2-1	Entering records into a datasheet (This objective is also covered in Topic B.)
AC03S-4-2	Using datasheet, Pivot Chart, Web page, and layout views This objective is also covered in: • Topic B of this unit • The unit titled "Working with reports" • *Access 2003: Intermediate*, in the units titled "Internet integration" and "PivotTables and PivotCharts"

Creating a table

Explanation

After creating a database, you need to create tables in which to store the data. You can create a table in three ways:

- By using the Table Wizard
- By using Design view
- By using Datasheet view

After creating a table, you can add fields to it and set the primary key. A *primary key* in is a field that uniquely identifies each record in a table. For example, you can use a separate number for each retailer; these numbers will identify the retailers uniquely. After you've created a table by using the Table Wizard, you can modify field names, data types, field sizes, or other field properties in Design view.

Using the Table Wizard

The Table Wizard provides two categories of sample tables: one with 25 common business tables, and the other with 20 common tables for personal use. Each sample table contains a set of sample fields. You can create a table by adding the sample fields of your choice.

To create a table by using the Table Wizard:

1. Open the database for which you want to create a table. In the Objects bar, click Tables.
2. Select the Create table by using wizard option, and click Open to open the Table Wizard dialog box.
3. In the Table Wizard dialog box, select a table category (Business or Personal) to view the list of sample tables in that category, as shown in Exhibit 2-4.
4. From the Sample Tables list, select a sample table.
5. From the Sample Fields list, select sample fields for the table you're creating.
6. Set the primary key for the table, and click Finish.

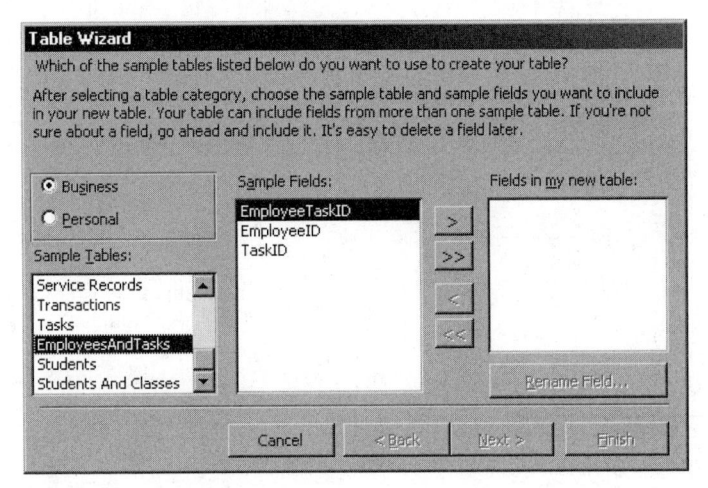

Exhibit 2-4: The Table Wizard

Access 2003: Basic

Do it!

C-1: Creating a table by using the Table Wizard

Here's how	Here's why
1 Open CreateDatabase	In the current unit folder.
2 On the Objects bar, verify that Tables is selected	
3 Select **Create table by using wizard**	You'll create a table by using the Table Wizard.
4 Click **Open**	The first dialog box of the Table Wizard appears. By default, Business is selected.
5 From the Sample Tables list, select **EmployeesAndTasks**	This is a predefined sample table containing some sample fields. You can reuse this table and its fields instead of creating your own. The Sample Fields list shows all the fields of the EmployeesAndTasks table. Notice that the field EmployeeTaskID is selected.
6 Click **>**	To add the field EmployeeTaskID to the Fields in my new table list.
7 Click **>>**	To add all the fields to the Fields in my new table list.
Observe the fields in the list Fields in my new table	Notice that an extra field, EmployeeTaskID1, is added to the list, along with the remaining fields of the sample table. This extra field is selected.
Click **<**	To remove this field from the Fields in my new table list.
8 Click **Next**	To display the next dialog box of the Table Wizard.
9 Edit the What do you want to name your table box to read **tblEmployeeTasks**	To name the table.
10 Select **No, I'll set the primary key.**	You'll set the primary key manually.
Click **Next**	To display the next dialog box of the Table Wizard.
11 From the What field will hold data that is unique for each record list, select **EmployeeID**, as shown	EmployeeTaskID ▼ EmployeeTaskID **EmployeeID** TaskID
	This will be the primary key for the table.

12	Verify that the option is selected as shown	⦿ Consecutive numbers Microsoft Access assigns automatically to new records. ○ Numbers I enter when I add new records. ○ Numbers and/or letters I enter when I add new records.
		To generate employee codes automatically.
	Click **Next**	To display the next dialog box of the Table Wizard.
13	Verify that the option is selected as shown	○ Modify the table design. ⦿ Enter data directly into the table. ○ Enter data into the table using a form the wizard creates for me.
		Use this option to see the table in Datasheet view and add or edit data.
14	Click **Finish**	To open the tblEmployeeTasks : Table window.
	Observe the screen	You'll see the tblEmployeeTasks table in Datasheet view. Under EmployeeID, AutoNumber appears, which means that Access will automatically generate Employee IDs for the employees.
15	Close the table	Choose File, Close.

Creating tables in Design view

Explanation

To create a table in Design view:

1. Open the database for which you want to create the table.
2. On the Objects bar, click Tables.
3. Select the Create table in Design view option, and then click Open to open the table in Design view.

You can then enter the necessary information, such as adding a field name and description in the Field and Description columns. Another column, Data Type, contains a drop-down arrow that you can use to select a data type from the list.

The following table describes some of the data types, along with the size and type of data they can store:

Data type	Size	Type of data it stores
Text	Up to 255 characters.	Text information or combinations of text and numbers, such as an address, a name, or a phone number.
Number	Several sizes available to store numbers with varying degrees of precision.	Numeric information used in calculations.
Date/Time	Accommodates dates and time across thousands of years.	Dates and times, such as 2/3/2000 2:00:00 PM and 1/1/2150 5:00:00 PM.
Currency	Up to 15 digits to the left of the decimal point and 4 digits to the right.	Monetary values, such as $5.00.
Yes/No	Size controlled by Access.	Stores one of the two values: Yes or No.
Memo	Up to 65,535 characters.	Lengthy text such as comments or notes.

Design view contains a row selector, which indicates the active row with a black triangle, as shown in Exhibit 2-5. The lower pane is the Field Properties pane, which contains two tabs: General and Lookup. Use the General tab to set field properties, such as the size of a field. Use the Lookup tab to modify field properties, such as the appearance of a field in a table.

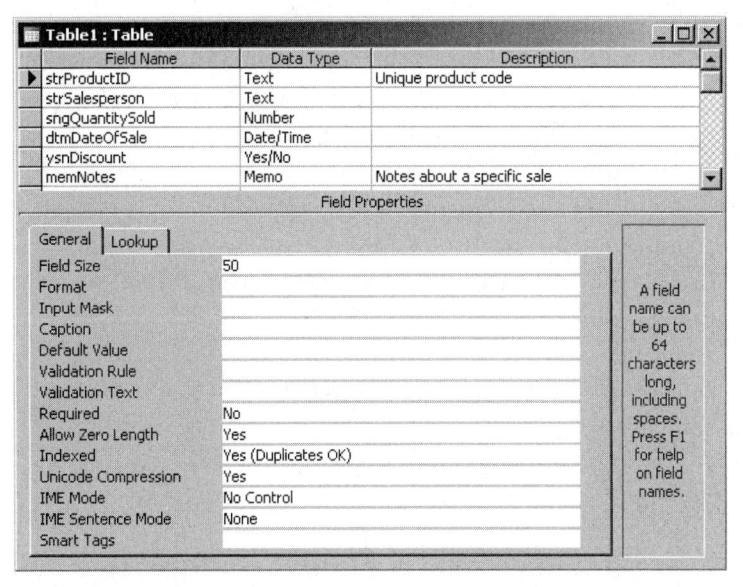

Exhibit 2-5: A table in Design view

Do it!

C-2: Creating a table in Design view

Here's how	Here's why
1 Verify that Tables is selected	(On the Objects bar.) You'll create a table in this database by using Design view.
2 Select **Create table in Design view**	
3 Click **Open**	To open the table in Design view.
4 Observe the window title	The title Table1 : Table appears.
Observe the upper pane of the window	The row selector is positioned to the left of the first record.
Observe the Field Properties pane	This pane has two tabs: General and Lookup. By default, the General tab is activated.

Adding fields

Explanation

You can use various data types, such as Text or Number, depending on the type of data the field should store. For example, if you want to store addresses or ZIP codes that contain characters, numbers, or a combination of both, you can choose the Text data type.

1. In Design view, place the insertion point in the Field Name column, and enter a name for the field.
2. Press Tab to move to the Data Type column. Click the drop-down arrow, and select Text from the Data Type list.
3. Press Tab to move to the Description column. Enter a description of the field.

The default size of a text field is 50 characters. However, you can change the field size by using the General tab of the Field Properties pane. You can't assign the Text data type to a field if you want to enter a date in it or perform calculations. In such cases, you assign such data types as Date/Time or Number.

Sometimes, you might want to store long text data, which might include characters and numbers. For example, you might want to store notes on a specific sale. In that case, you can use a field with the Memo data type.

To add fields of any data type to your table, you enter the field name in the Field Name column and select the data type from the Data Type list.

Do it!

C-3: Adding fields and descriptions to a table

Here's how	Here's why
1 In the Field Name column, enter **strProductID**	This is the name of the first field in the table.
2 Press `TAB`	To move to the Data Type column. You'll see a drop-down arrow.
Click the drop-down arrow	To display the Data Type list. By default, Text is selected. This will be the data type for the field strProductID.
Click the drop-down arrow again	To close the list.
3 Press `TAB`	To move to the Description column.
4 In the Description column, enter **Unique product code**	

Databases and tables **2–23**

5 In the Field Name column, place the insertion point in the second row	To enter the second field. The row selector moves to the next field row.
Enter **strSalesperson**	This is the name of the second field.
Press TAB	To move to the Data Type column. Text is selected as the data type.
6 In the Field Name column, place the insertion point in the third row	You'll add another field to the table.
Enter **sngQuantitySold**	This is the name of the third field.
Press TAB	You'll select a data type for the sngQuantitySold field.
From Data Type list, select **Number**	
7 Add the field **dtmDateOfSale**	This field will store the date on which a sale was made.
From Data Type list, select **Date/Time**	This will be the data type for the dtmDateOfSale field.
8 Add the field **ysnDiscount**	This field will store the status of the availability of discounts for specific products.
From Data Type list, select **Yes/No**	This will be the data type for the Discount field.
9 Add the field **memNotes**	This will be the sixth field. It will store details about sales.
From the Data Type list, select **Memo**	To assign a Memo data type for the field.
In the Description column, enter **Notes about a specific sale**	

Setting the primary key for a table

Explanation

Sometimes, you might find that two records in a table have the same value, making it difficult to differentiate among them. For example, a field called strSalesperson could store duplicate values if two or more salespeople have the same name. In that case, you could use a field called strSalespersonID as the primary key, and it would store a unique value for each salesperson.

To set a field as a primary key, either place the insertion point in the cell or select the field, and do any of the following:

- Choose Edit, Primary Key.
- Click the Primary Key button on the Table Design toolbar.
- Right-click the field row, and select Primary Key from the shortcut menu.

Do it!

C-4: Setting the primary key

Here's how	Here's why
1 In the Field Name column, place the insertion point in the first row	You'll set the field strProductID as the primary key.
2 Click	(The Primary Key button is on the Table Design toolbar.) A key icon appears to the left of strProductID to show that strProductID is now the primary key.

Databases and tables   **2–25**

Saving and viewing tables

Explanation   After you have completed the table design, you need to save it. You can save a table by choosing File, Save As or by choosing File, Save. By choosing File, Save As, you can save a table with a different name. You can also save a table by clicking the Save button on the Table Design or Table Datasheet toolbar. You need to provide a name for the table before saving it for the first time. After you save the table, you can open it in Datasheet view and enter data.

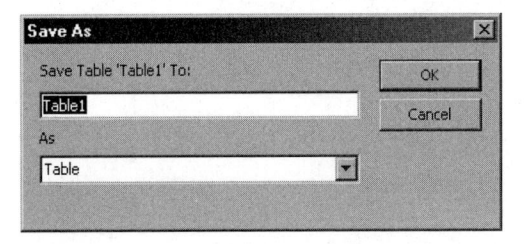

Exhibit 2-6: The Save As dialog box

Do it!   ### C-5:   Saving the design and viewing the table

Here's how	Here's why
1 Choose **File, Save As…**	To open the Save As dialog box, as shown in Exhibit 2-6.
Edit the Save Table 'Table1' To box to read **tblSales**	You'll save the table as tblSales.
In the As list, verify that Table is selected	
Click **OK**	(To save the table.) The name on the table title bar changes to tblSales : Table.
Close the Design window	The table tblSales appears in the Database window.
2 Select **tblSales**	
Click **Open**	To open the tblSales : Table window in Datasheet view.
3 Observe the column headings	The column headings are the same as the field names you entered in Design view.
Observe the first row	The row selector is positioned to the left of the first row.

Adding records

Explanation

After you create and save a table, you can enter data in it. To do so, you need to open the table in Datasheet view. When you enter data into a record, Access automatically saves the record.

There are three ways to enter data in a table:
- Click the New Record button on the Table Datasheet toolbar.
- Click the new record navigation button.
- Place the insertion point in the row under the first field heading, and enter data.

Do it!

C-6: Adding a record

Here's how	Here's why
1 In the strProductID column, enter **1**	strProductID 1 This is the product ID for the first product.
2 Press TAB	To move to the next field.
3 In the strSalesperson column, enter **Bill MacArthur**	strSalesperson Bill MacArthur This is the salesperson's name for the first record.
4 Edit the sngQuantitySold column to read **30**	
5 In the dtmDateOfSale column, enter **01/01/03**	dtmDateOfSale 1/1/2003
6 In the ysnDiscount column, check as shown	ysnDiscount ☑
7 In the memNotes column, enter **Credit card no. 9696-1504-8900-3423**	memNotes Credit card no. 9696-1504-8900-3423
8 Choose **File, Close**	A message box will appear if you increased the column width of the memNotes field in a previous step. The message box prompts you to confirm the change in the layout (design) before saving.
Click **No**	(If necessary) To close the table without saving the changes made for memNotes field.
9 Close CreateDatabase	Choose File, Close.

Unit summary: Databases and tables

Topic A In this topic, you learned how to **plan a database**. You learned that you need to follow the **naming rules** while creating a database and its objects. You also learned how to create a database by using the **Database Wizard**. In addition, you learned how to **create a blank database**. You learned that you have more flexibility when creating a blank database.

Topic B In this topic, you learned how to use various views, such as **Design** and **Datasheet**. You learned that you can use Datasheet view to scroll through records, and use Design view to modify a table's design. You also learned how to **examine** a **table** in Datasheet view and in Design view.

Topic C In this topic, you learned how to create a table by using the **Table Wizard** and how to modify a table in Design view. You also learned how to set the **primary key**. In addition, you learned how to create a table in **Design view**. You also learned how to add **Text, Number, Date/Time, Yes/No,** and **Memo fields** to a new table. You also learned how to set the primary key in Design view and how to **save** a table. In addition, you learned how to **add a record** to a new table.

Independent practice activity

1 Plan and design a database for storing information about customers who place orders for different products. The database should have a minimum of two tables.

2 Create a new blank database with a name of your choice.

3 Create a table by using the Table Wizard.

4 Select a sample table of your choice.

5 Select sample fields, and set a primary key.

6 Click Finish to close the Table Wizard.

7 Create a table in Design view, set the primary key, and save the table as tblCustomerOrder, as shown in Exhibit 2-7.

8 Enter data in tblCustomerOrder as shown in Exhibit 2-8.

9 Save and close the table.

10 Close the database.

tblCustomerOrder : Table

	Field Name	Data Type	Description
🔑▶	lngOrderNo	AutoNumber	Order number, automatically generated by Access
	strProductID	Text	Product identification number
	dtmOrderDate	Date/Time	Date the order was placed
	strCustomer	Text	Name of customer who placed the order
	lngOrderQuantity	Number	Quantity of product ordered by customer
	ysnDispatched	Yes/No	If the order has already dispatched

Exhibit 2-7: The tblCustomerOrder table in Design view after Step 7 of the Independent Practice Activity

	lngOrderNo	strProductID	dtmOrderDate	strCustomer	lngOrderQuantit	ysnDispatched
	1	1	1/2/2003	Rebecca Austin	250	☑
	2	2	2/2/2003	Annie Philips	367	☑
	3	3	12/3/2003	Julie Stone	234	☐
▶	(AutoNumber)				0	▩

Exhibit 2-8: The records in the tblCustomerOrder table after Step 8 of the Independent Practice Activity

Review questions

1 Why would you use the Database Wizard to create a database?

2 What is the advantage of creating a database manually without using the Database Wizard?

3 Which of the following views displays data in a tabular format containing rows and columns?

A Design view

B Datasheet view

C Chart view

D Pivot Table view

4 Which view is used to add field details?

5 In Datasheet view, how do you move between records?

6 The Table Wizard helps you create tables from which two categories?

   A Business and Economic

   B Educational and Personal

   C Business and Personal

   D Business and Statistical

7 Which view is used to enter data in a table?

Unit 3
Fields and records

Unit time: 50 minutes

Complete this unit, and you'll know how to:

A Modify the table design by modifying field names, inserting and deleting fields, and moving fields.

B Use the Find feature and the spelling checker in a table.

C Sort, filter, and delete records.

Topic A: Changing the design of a table

This topic covers the following Microsoft Office Specialist exam objectives.

#	Objective
AC03S-1-2	Modifying table properties or structure (This objective is also covered in the unit titled "Databases and tables.")
AC03S-1-3	Modifying field types (This objective is also covered in the unit titled "Databases and tables.")

Effective field names

Explanation

After you create a table, you might decide that a field isn't relevant and needs to be deleted. You might also find that you need to insert new fields in the table, change field names, or change the order in which fields appear. You can do these things by modifying the table in Design view.

You and others will have an easier time using your database if you give each field a name that reflects its purpose. For example, the field name ProductName is easier to understand than the field name Pname.

To make the field names clear and readable, you should use a combination of uppercase and lowercase letters. Exhibit 3-1 shows a table with field names that are not very meaningful.

Field Name	Data Type	Description
PrID	AutoNumber	Unique ID automatically assigned to each new product
Pname	Text	Full name of product as it appears in catalog
Up	Currency	Price of each unit of product
strUnit	Text	Bulk amount or container size
Discount	Yes/No	Discount given or not

Exhibit 3-1: A table with uninformative field names

Changing field names

Ideally, the name of a field should be self-explanatory. You can change any field name in Design view. Changing the field name does not affect the existing data in the table.

Fields and records **3–3**

It's also helpful if you use consistent naming conventions and names that reflect both the field's data type and its purpose. The following table shows some examples:

Data type	Purpose	Field name
Text (string)	Employee last name	strEmpLastName
Memo	Product description	memItemDesc
Number (long integer)	Employee number	lngEmpID
Date	Shipping date	dtmShipDate
Currency	Product cost	curProductCost
Hyperlink	Supplier Web site	hypSupplierHome

Do it!

A-1: Modifying field names

Here's how	Here's why
1 Open WorkingWithRecords	(From the current unit folder.) You'll view the design of a table in this database.
2 In the Objects bar, verify that Tables is selected	
Select **tblProduct**	
Click **Design**	(To open the table in Design view.) You'll analyze the design of this table.
3 Under the Field Name column, observe the field names PrID and Pname	You'll change the field names to make them more self-explanatory.
4 Select **PrID**	(If necessary.) You'll change the name of the first field.
Enter **lngProductID**	This will be the new name for the first field.
5 Change the other field names as shown	Field Name: lngProductID, strProductName, curUnitPrice, strUnit, ysnDiscount
6 Update the table	Choose File, Save.

Deleting and inserting fields in a table

Explanation

After you have created a table, you might find that you need to add or delete fields. You must first select a field to delete it or to insert a record over it.

Selecting a field

You can select a field by clicking its row selector, as shown in Exhibit 3-2. When you move the pointer over the row selector, it changes to an arrow. You can now delete this field or insert a new field above it.

Field Name	Data Type	Description
lngProductID	AutoNumber	Unique ID automatically assigned to each new product
strProductName	Text	Full name of product as it appears in catalog
curUnitPrice	Currency	Price of each unit of product
strUnit	Text	Bulk amount or container size
ysnDiscount	Yes/No	Discount given or not

Exhibit 3-2: A table with a selected field

Deleting a field

To delete a field in Design view, you must select the field and then either press the Delete key or choose Edit, Delete. For example, in the tblProduct table, if you want to delete the ysnDiscount field, first select the field, as shown in Exhibit 3-2, and then delete it. Before you can delete a field, Access will prompt you to confirm the deletion if the field contains data or if the field is a primary key. Access will not prompt you if the field is empty.

Inserting a field

In Design view, you can insert a field either at the end of the table or above an existing field. To insert a field above an existing field, select the field above which you want to insert the new field, and choose Insert, Rows. To add a new field at the end, select the first empty field row.

Do it!

A-2: Deleting and inserting fields

Here's how	Here's why
1 Click the row selector for the ysnDiscount field as shown	➡ ysnDiscount Yes/No To select the field.
2 Choose **Edit**, **Delete**	A message box appears asking you to confirm the deletion.
Click **Yes**	To delete the ysnDiscount field from the table.
3 Under Field Name, place the insertion point in the field **curUnitPrice**	You'll insert a field above this field.
4 Choose **Insert**, **Rows**	(A blank row appears above the field curUnitPrice.) The insertion point is in the first cell of the new row.
Under Field Name, in the inserted row, enter **sngMinQuantity**	(To specify the new field name.) This field stores data for the minimum quantity to be stored for each product.
Under Data Type, enter select **Number**	
Under Description, enter **Minimum quantity stored**	
5 Update the table	

Moving fields

Explanation

If you enter the field details in an unsuitable sequence when you create a table, you might need to rearrange the fields by moving the field rows in Design view.

To move a field row:

1. Select the field row by using the row selector.
2. Point to the left side of the selected row.
3. Click and hold the mouse button. The appearance of the pointer changes to an arrow with a box, as shown in Exhibit 3-3.
4. Drag the field row to the location where you want to place it. The field row in that position automatically shifts down to the next row.

Exhibit 3-3: The pointer when moving a field

Do it!

A-3: Moving a field

Here's how	Here's why
1 Select the row for the field sngMinQuantity	(Click the row selector for the field sngMinQuantity.) You'll move this field below the field strUnit.
Click and hold the mouse button while pointing to the left of the selected row	(As shown in Exhibit 3-3.) The mouse pointer changes to an arrow with a box, indicating that you can now drag the field to a new location.
2 Drag to the row below strUnit	(When you see a heavy black line below strUnit, you'll know you're moving the row to the correct position.) The entire row for sngMinQuantity is moved here.
3 Update the table	
4 Close the table	

Topic B: Finding and editing records

Explanation

Scrolling through a large table to find specific records is not practical. You can use the Find feature to locate records that meet criteria you enter. You can also use Find to locate data values and replace them with different values.

Sometimes, you might accidentally delete or modify some values in a record when entering data. To restore the original values without reentering the data, use the Undo button on the Table Datasheet toolbar.

Finding and replacing values

To search for a value in a field, place the insertion point on the first data value in the specified field, and then click the Find button on the Table Datasheet toolbar or choose Edit, Find. Use the Find and Replace dialog box, shown in Exhibit 3-4, to specify the values you want to find. This dialog box contains two tabs: Find and Replace. In the Find tab, you can specify the value you want to find. In the Replace tab, you can specify a value with which you want to replace it.

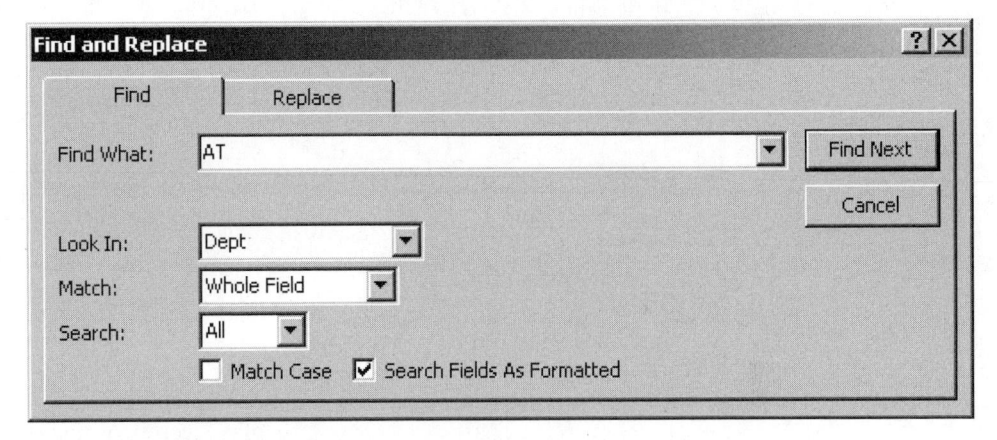

Exhibit 3-4: The Find and Replace dialog box

Access 2003: Basic

Do it!

B-1: Finding and replacing a value

Here's how	Here's why
1 Open tblEmployee	This table contains information about employees. You'll find occurrences of the department code AT and replace them with AC.
2 Place the insertion point in the first data value in the Dept field	You'll search for a specific value in this field.
3 Click [binoculars icon]	(The Find button is on the Table Datasheet toolbar.) To open the Find and Replace dialog box. By default, the Find tab is activated.
In the Find What box, enter **AT**	To find this value in the Dept field.
In the Look In list, verify that Dept is selected	To specify that the value is to be searched for in the Dept field.
In the Match list, verify that Whole Field is selected	To specify that the search needs to be done with the entire field.
In the Search list, verify that All is selected	To specify that the entire table needs to be searched.
Click **Find Next**	The first occurrence of AT, corresponding to the employee Shannon Lee, is highlighted.
4 Click the **Replace** tab	
In the Replace With box, enter **AC**	
Click **Replace**	(To replace AT with AC.) The next occurrence of AT, corresponding to the employee Melissa James, is automatically highlighted.
Click **Replace All**	To replace the remaining occurrences of AT without prompting each time.
Click **Yes**	To confirm that you won't be able to undo this operation.
5 Click **Cancel**	To close the Find and Replace dialog box.
Observe the values in the Dept field	All five instances of AT have been replaced with AC.

Fields and records   **3–9**

Undoing changes in a table

Explanation   If you accidentally delete or modify a record, you can use the Undo button on the Table Datasheet toolbar to restore the deleted or modified values. You can also choose Edit, Undo. However, you can undo only the most recently changed value.

Do it!   **B-2: Undoing changes**

Here's how	Here's why
1 In the Earnings column, select the first data value	
Press DELETE	(To delete the value.) You'll check if this value can be restored.
2 Click ↶	(The Undo button is on the Table Datasheet toolbar.) To restore the deleted value.
3 Close the table	Do not save changes.

The spelling checker

Explanation

You can use the spelling checker to find and correct any misspelled words in a text or memo field. To check spelling, select the columns or fields you want to check, and choose Tools, Spelling. Access uses a built-in dictionary to check the spelling of words. If Access finds any words that are not in the dictionary, the spelling checker offers one or more suggestions for replacements, as shown in Exhibit 3-5. In the Spelling dialog box, you can either accept a suggestion by selecting the suggested word and clicking Change, or ignore the suggestion and continue with the spelling check by clicking Ignore. Clicking Add will add that word to the dictionary so it won't be flagged again.

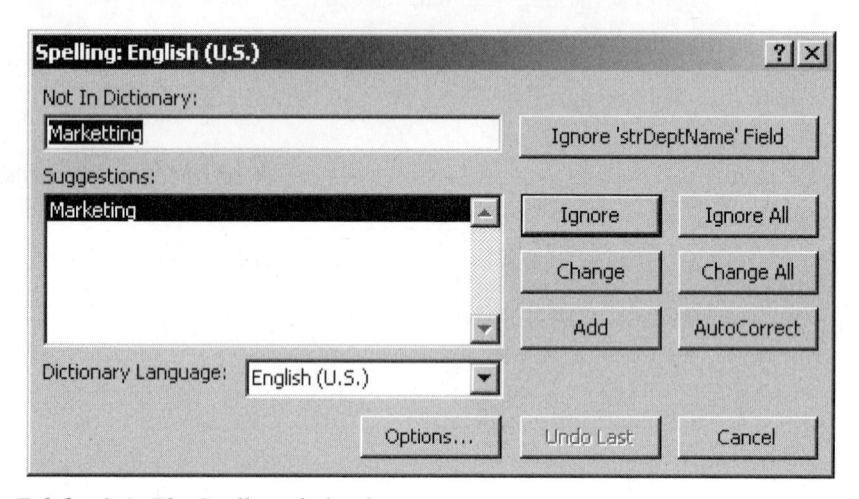

Exhibit 3-5: The Spelling dialog box

Fields and records **3-11**

Do it!

B-3: Using the spelling checker

Here's how	Here's why
1 Open tblDept	
2 Click on the field heading for Dept Name, as shown	

Dept Code	↓ Dept Name
▶ AC	Accounting
AD	Administration
CS	Customer Service
HR	Human Resources
MK	Marketting
PR	Purchasing
QC	Quality Control
SH	Shipping
SL	Sales
*	

(To select the Dept Name column.) You'll check the spelling in the Dept Name column.

3 Choose **Tools**, **Spelling...** (To open the Spelling dialog box, as shown in Exhibit 3-5.) The spelling of "Marketing" (as "Marketting") in the Dept Name field is identified as incorrect.

4 In the Spelling dialog box, click **Change** (To accept the suggested spelling.) A message box appears indicating that the spelling check is complete and that there are no more spelling errors.

5 Click **OK** To close the message box.

In the Dept Name field, observe the value for the Dept Code MK The spelling is corrected.

6 Update and close the table

Topic C: Organizing records

This topic covers the following Microsoft Office Specialist exam objectives.

#	Objective
AC03S-3-5	Sorting records in tables, queries, forms and reports (This objective is also covered in the units titled "Simple queries," "Using forms," and "Working with reports.")
AC03S-3-6	Filtering datasheets by form (This objective is also covered in the unit titled "Using forms.")
AC03S-3-6	Filtering datasheets by selection

Sorting and filtering

Explanation

You can organize records by sorting, filtering, and deleting them. *Sorting* is the process of organizing records in a meaningful way so that you can retrieve data in an order of your choice. For example, if you want to view records in the ascending order of the last names of employees, you can sort the records based on the values in the last-name field. You can sort records based on one or more fields.

Filtering is the process of temporarily isolating a subset of records that satisfy certain criteria you specify. For example, suppose that you want to delete or edit Human Resources department records in Datasheet view without navigating through the records of all the departments. To do this, you can filter the Human Resources department records to isolate them from the table containing the records of all the departments. You can also format and print the filtered records. Access provides several methods for filtering, such as Filter By Selection, Filter By Form, Filter Excluding Selection, and Advanced Filter/Sort.

Sorting records by a single field in a table

Records in a table are automatically sorted based on the primary key field. However, you might want to sort the records based on a different field. The maximum number of characters for a sort field (or fields) is 255. You can sort in either ascending or descending order.

To sort a field in ascending order, select the field, and then choose Records, Sort, Sort Ascending, or click the relevant Sort button on the Table Datasheet toolbar.

You can also right-click the field and choose Sort Ascending or Sort Descending from the shortcut menu. In ascending sort order, text values will be sorted alphabetically from A to Z, and date values will be sorted from the earliest to the latest. Number or currency values will be sorted from the lowest value to the highest.

Do it!

C-1: Sorting records by a single field

Here's how	Here's why
1 Open tblEmployee	
2 Select the Last Name column	You'll sort records in the First Name field in ascending order.
3 Choose **Records**, **Sort**, **Sort Ascending**	(To sort the records in ascending order.) The records are sorted in ascending order based on the First Name field.

Sorting records by multiple fields in a table

Explanation

You can sort records based on more than one field by selecting the fields and choosing Records, Sort, Sort Ascending (or Sort Descending). The fields must be adjacent to each other in Datasheet view. The sort fields have precedence from left to right. For example, if you select the fields Dept and Hire Date from left to right, the records will be sorted based first on Dept and then on Hire Date.

Selecting and sorting multiple fields

To select two fields, click the field heading to select the first column. Then, drag to the right or left to select the adjacent column. Both columns will be highlighted, as shown in Exhibit 3-6. Then choose Records, Sort, Sort Ascending (or Sort Descending) to sort the records.

If you want to select more than two fields, drag until you reach the necessary number of columns. You'll see that all the selected columns are highlighted.

Last Name	Dept	Hire Date
Long	AD	6/20/2001
Morris	AC	5/6/2002
Philips	SH	9/12/2002
Roberts	SL	3/4/2003
Owens	MK	2/22/2002
Overmire	AD	9/19/1999
Morrison	SH	1/15/2003
Bennet	SL	12/17/1994
James	AC	4/2/1995
Meyers	AD	12/5/2002
Pingault	SH	2/14/2001
Smith	AD	6/15/1989

Exhibit 3-6: The tblEmployee table with multiple columns selected for sorting

Do it!

C-2: Sorting records by multiple fields

Here's how	Here's why
1 Point to the field heading Dept	
Click and hold the mouse button	To select the field Dept.
Drag to the right, as shown	Dept	Hire Date
	AD	6/20/2001
	AC	5/6/2002
	SH	9/12/2002
	SL	3/4/2003
	MK	2/22/2002
	AD	9/19/1999
	SH	1/15/2003
	SL	12/17/1994
	(To select both fields, Dept and Hire Date, for sorting.) You'll sort records based on these two fields.
2 Choose **Records**, **Sort**, **Sort Ascending**	The records are arranged in ascending order, based first on Dept and then on Hire Date. The records are no longer sorted based on First Name.
3 Close the table	Do not save changes.

Filtering records by using Filter By Selection

Explanation

In Datasheet view, you can use the Filter By Selection feature to display records based on a field value. For example, if you want to view the records of the Accounting department, you can apply a filter so that only records from the AC department appear in the table, as shown in Exhibit 3-7.

To filter records by using Filter By Selection, first place the insertion point next to the field value by which you want to filter the records. Then choose Records, Filter, Filter By Selection.

tblEmployee : Table						
Emp ID	Emp HR#	First Name	Last Name	Dept	Hire Date	Earnings
2	04-28973	Shannon	Lee	AC	2/20/1998	$76,600.00
7	11-49618	Melissa	James	AC	3/1/2002	$53,500.00
16	04-37861	Kendra	James	AC	4/2/1995	$65,000.00
25	04-89161	Pamela	Carter	AC	3/30/2002	$80,000.00
26	05-89165	Anna	Morris	AC	5/6/2002	$47,500.00

Exhibit 3-7: The tblEmployee table with records filtered on the AC department

Do it!

C-3: Using Filter By Selection

Here's how	Here's why
1 Open tblEmployee	
2 In the Dept column, select the value **AC** in any row	You'll filter records for this value.
3 Choose **Records**, **Filter**, **Filter By Selection**	To filter records for the department AC. Notice that only the records that contain the Department value AC appear in the table, as shown in Exhibit 3-7.
4 Choose **Records, Remove Filter/Sort**	To remove the filter and the sort. Notice that the records are no longer sorted or filtered.
5 Close the table	Do not save changes.

Fields and records

Filtering records by using Filter By Form

Explanation The Filter By Form feature helps you filter records based on a specific condition. When you use the Filter By Form feature in a table in Datasheet view, a table with empty fields appears. You can enter values in these empty fields to specify the filtering criteria.

To filter records by using Filter By Form, choose Records, Filter, Filter By Form or click the Filter By Form button on the Table Datasheet toolbar. Then enter the criteria in the empty fields.

Do it! **C-4: Using Filter By Form**

Here's how	Here's why
1 Open tblEmployee	
2 Choose **Records**, **Filter**, **Filter By Form**	A table with empty fields appears.
3 In the first row, under Earnings, enter as shown	Dept | Hire Date | Earnings 　　　|　　　　| >50000 You'll display the records of employees whose earnings are greater than $50,000.
4 Choose **Filter**, **Apply Filter/Sort**	To apply the filter. Notice that only the records of employees whose earnings are greater than $50,000 appear.
5 Remove the filter	Choose Records, Remove Filter/Sort.

Access 2003: Basic

Filtering records by using Filter Excluding Selection

Explanation

You use the Filter Excluding Selection feature to filter out (exclude) records containing a specific value. For example, you can use this feature to display the records of all employees except for those in the Accounting department.

To filter records by using Filter Excluding Selection, place the insertion point next to the data value you want to filter, and then choose Records, Filter, Filter Excluding Selection.

Do it!

C-5: Using Filter Excluding Selection

Here's how	Here's why
1 Place the insertion point as shown	Dept SH AC CS You'll apply a filter to this value.
2 Choose **Records**, **Filter**, **Filter Excluding Selection**	To apply the filter. The table displays the records of all employees *except* those in the AC department.
3 Remove the filter	
4 Close the table	Do not save changes.

Filtering records by using Advanced Filter/Sort

Explanation

When you use the Advanced Filter/Sort feature, you specify the criteria to filter records in a design grid. This feature helps you search for records that satisfy any specific or multiple criteria.

To filter records by using Advanced Filter/Sort, choose Records, Filter, Advanced Filter/Sort to open the design grid. Then, specify the criteria for filtering the records.

Do it!

C-6: Using Advanced Filter/Sort

Here's how	Here's why
1 Open tblProduct	
2 Choose **Records**, **Filter**, **Advanced Filter/Sort...**	(To open the design grid.) The tblProduct table appears in the upper pane of the design grid. The insertion point is in the first column of the field row.
3 In the Field row, select from the list as shown	
	To add the strUnit field to the design grid.
Place the insertion point in the second column of the Field row	You'll add a field to the second column of the Field row.
From the list, select **curUnitPrice**	To add this field to the design grid.
4 Place the insertion point in the first column of the Criteria row	You'll specify a criterion for the field strUnit.
Enter **> 2 oz**	To view the details of products whose unit value is greater than 2 oz.
5 Place the insertion point in the second column of the criteria row	To specify a criterion for the field curUnitPrice.
Enter **> 1.5**	To view the details of products whose unit price is greater than $1.50.
6 Choose **Filter**, **Apply Filter/Sort**	The table displays the records of the products whose current unit price is greater than $1.50 and whose unit value is greater than 2 oz.
7 Remove the filter	

Deleting records

Explanation

You might want to delete one or more records from a table to ensure that the table contains the latest information. For example, if you are not currently selling a specific product, you might need to delete that product's record. To do this, select the record and either choose Edit, Delete or press the Delete key.

You can also place the insertion point anywhere in the record and choose Edit, Delete Record.

The difference between choosing Edit, Delete and Edit, Delete Record is that, in the first method, you must select the record, and in the second, you only need to place the insertion point in any of columns of the record you want to delete. After a record is deleted, it cannot be restored.

Selecting a record

To select a record, click its record selector. The record will be highlighted, as shown in Exhibit 3-8.

Exhibit 3-8: A table with a selected record

Do it!

C-7: Deleting a record

Here's how	Here's why
1 Click as shown	The fourth record contains the details for Celery Seed (Ground). Notice that the record selector appears next to the selected record.
2 Choose **Edit**, **Delete**	(To delete the fourth record in the tblProduct table.) A message box appears prompting you to confirm the deletion.
3 Click **Yes**	The fourth record in the table is deleted.
4 Update and close the table	
5 Close the database	

Unit summary: Fields and records

Topic A In this topic, you learned how to **modify the table design** by changing the name of a **field**, deleting and inserting fields, and moving fields.

Topic B In this topic, you learned how to use the **Find and Replace** dialog box to find and replace values in a table. You learned how to **undo** changes that you have made in a record. You also learned how to use the **spelling checker** to find and correct any misspelled words in a table.

Topic C In this topic, you learned how to **sort** records based on single or multiple fields. You learned how to sort records in the ascending or descending order of any field. You also learned how to view selected records by applying a **filter**. You filtered records by using various methods, such as Filter By Selection, Filter By Form, Filter Excluding Selection, and Advanced Filter/Sort.

Independent practice activity

1 Open ModifyingDatabase. Then, open the table tblNewRetailer in Design view and observe its design.

2 Open the table tblRetailer in Design view and observe its design. Compare it to the design of tblNewRetailer.

3 Modify the design of the tblRetailer table so that it matches the tblNewRetailer table, as shown in Exhibit 3-9. Save the design changes.

4 Close the tblRetailer table, and maximize the tblNewRetailer table.

5 Switch to Datasheet view, and check the spelling of the City field in all records.

6 Sort the records by First Name in ascending order.

7 Use Filter By Selection to filter records whose Region field contains the value NY.

8 Remove the filter.

9 Use Filter By Form to filter records whose City field contains the value Portland.

10 Save and close the tblNewRetailer table.

11 Open the tblProduct table.

12 Use Advanced Filter/Sort to find products whose unit price is greater than $5.00.

13 Save and close the table and the database.

Field Name	Data Type	Description
lngRetailerID	AutoNumber	Unique ID automatically assigned to each Retailer
strRetailerName	Text	Full name of Retailer
strAddr1	Text	Address Line 1 of Retailer
strAddr2	Text	Address Line 2 of Retailer
strCity	Text	Retailer's City
strRegion	Text	Retailer's State or Province (use std mailing abbreviation)
strPostalCode	Text	Retailer's Zip or Postal Code (use Zip+4 if possible)
strFirstName	Text	First name of purchasing agent at the Retailer
strLastName	Text	Last name of purchasing agent at the Retailer
strPhone	Text	Retailer's Voice Phone and extension
strFax	Text	Retailer's Fax number
lngRep	Number	Company Account Representative ID for this Retailer

Exhibit 3-9: The tblNewRetailer table design

Review questions

1 Which view is used to change the name of a field?

   A Design view

   B Layout view

   C Field view

   D Datasheet view

2 What is the first step before inserting or deleting a field?

3 By default, where are new rows inserted?

4 When deleting a field, in which of the following instance are you *not* prompted to confirm the deletion?

   A The field contains data.

   B The field is the primary key.

   C The field is empty.

   D The field is a memo field.

5 What is the procedure to change a field name?

6 Which feature enables you to quickly locate records that meet specific criteria?

   A The Replace feature

   B The scrollbar

   C The Undo feature

   D The Find feature

7 What is the difference between sorting and filtering?

8 Name some of the ways to filter records.

9 When sorting records by multiple fields, which sort field takes precedence in the sort?

10 True or False? Deleted records can be restored.

Unit 4
Data entry rules

Unit time: 50 minutes

Complete this unit, and you'll know how to:

A Set properties for a field.

B Create input masks for fields, and use the Input Mask Wizard.

C Set validation rules for entering data in a field.

D Create single- and multiple-field indexes to sort and filter data in a table.

Topic A: Setting field properties

This topic covers the following Microsoft Office Specialist exam objective.

#	Objective
AC03S-1-4	Modifying field properties for tables in Table Design view

Field properties

Explanation

You can set properties for the fields in a table to control how data is stored and displayed in that table. For example, you can ensure that the Product ID field is never left blank or that data in the Postal Code field contains only five digits. Field properties are set in the Field Properties pane in Design view. You can set several properties for fields in a table. The following table describes some of these properties:

Property	Description
Required	Used to specify a field that cannot contain null values.
AllowZeroLength	Used to specify that the field can contain null values.
FieldSize	Used to specify the maximum number of characters that can be entered in the field.
SmartTags	Used to specify actions—such as sending e-mail, scheduling a meeting, or showing the calendar—for the data values in the fields.

The Required property

The *Required* property ensures that a field does not contain a null value. (A *null value* is a value that indicates missing or unknown data in a field.) If the Required property is set to Yes, you must enter a value in the field. To set this property for a field:

1. Open the table in Design view.
2. Display the general properties of the field that you want.
3. From the Required list, select Yes.
4. Update the table. A message box appears stating that you can test the existing data for the new rule that you have set.
5. Click No to skip testing the new rule on the existing data, or click Yes to test the new rule on the existing data.

Data entry rules **4-3**

Do it!

A-1: Setting the Required property

Here's how	Here's why
1 Open DataEntryRules	From the current unit folder.
2 Open tblRetailer	
3 Click [▶l]	(The last record button is at the bottom of the tblRetailer : Table window.) To move to the last record.
Under the Retailer Name column, enter **Magic Spices**	To specify the Retailer Name.
4 Click [▶*]	(The new record button is at the bottom of the tblRetailer : Table window.) To add another record to this table. Notice that you have not entered data in any other fields in the record.
5 Switch to Design view	
6 Place the insertion point as shown	Field Name lngRetailerID strRetailerName strAddr1|
	You'll set the Required property for the strAddr1 field. The general properties for the field strAddr1 appear in the General tab of the Field Properties pane.
7 From the Required list, select **Yes**	(In the Field Properties pane) To set the Required field property.
8 Update the table	A message appears prompting you to test the existing data for the rule that you created.
Click **No**	To skip testing the existing data for the new validation rule.
9 Switch to Datasheet view	You'll test the Required field property.

10	Add a new record	Click the new record button at the bottom of the tblRetailer : Table window.
	In the new record, under Retailer Name, enter **Spice Outlet**	
	Click [▶*]	(To add another new record.) A message box appears warning that you can't leave the field strAddr1 blank and prompting you to enter a value in the field. This is because the Required property has been set.
	Click **OK**	(To close the message box.) You'll enter a value in the Address1 field.
11	Press [TAB]	To move to the next cell.
	Enter **202 Brown St**	
12	Add a new record	The message box doesn't appear.
13	Delete the records with the Retailer Name Magic Spices and Spice Outlet	
14	Update the table	

The AllowZeroLength property

Explanation

You can set the *AllowZeroLength* property of a text, memo, or hyperlink field to make these fields accept strings of zero length. You can set the AllowZeroLength property with the Required property to ensure that no field is left blank by mistake. For example, if you set the Required property of an E-mail field to Yes, then data must be entered in that field. If you set the AllowZeroLength property to Yes, the field can contain values with no characters. You can then enter a null value (such as a space) in the E-mail field for those individuals who do not have an e-mail account.

To set the AllowZeroLength property for a field, display the general properties for the field. From the Allow Zero Length list, select Yes.

Data entry rules **4–5**

Do it! **A-2: Using the AllowZeroLength property**

Here's how	Here's why
1 Switch to Design view	
Display the general properties for the strPhone field	(Under Field Name, place the insertion point in the field strPhone.) You'll set the Required and AllowZeroLength properties of this field.
From the Required list, select **Yes**	To set the Required property.
From the Allow Zero Length list, select **Yes**	To set the AllowZeroLength property.
2 Update the table	A message box appears, stating that Access can test all the data in the table against the new rules.
Click **Yes**	To test the existing data and to save the table design.
3 Switch to Datasheet view	
4 Add a new record	
Under Retailer Name, enter **Magic Spices**	To specify the Retailer Name for the new record.
Under Address1, enter **111 SE Carnegie St**	
Under City, enter **Astoria**	
Under Region, enter **OR**	
Under Postal Code, enter **97102**	
5 Add a new record	A message appears stating that the strPhone field can't be left blank.
6 Click **OK**	To close the message box.
7 In the record for Retailer ID 0016, place the insertion point in the Phone field	You'll enter a null value in this column.
Press (SPACEBAR)	To specify a null value in the Phone column.
Add a new record	The warning message doesn't appear, which means that you can now enter null values in the Phone column. This ensures that you left the field blank on purpose.
8 Update the table	

The FieldSize property

Explanation

You use the *FieldSize* property to specify the maximum number of characters that can be entered in a field.

To set the FieldSize property, display the general properties for the field you want. In the Field Size box, enter the field size.

Do it!

A-3: Setting the FieldSize property

Here's how	Here's why
1 Switch to Design view Display the general properties for the field strPostalCode	
2 Edit the Field Size box to read **5**	To set the FieldSize property for the field.
3 Update the table	A message box appears stating that data might be lost because of the change in the FieldSize property.
Click **Yes**	To save the table so that the current values of this field do not exceed five characters.
4 Switch to Datasheet view Navigate to the last record	(Click the last record button at the bottom of the tblRetailer : Table window.) You'll enter a postal code in this record.
5 In the Postal Code field, select the value, as shown	CA 94111 TX 73344 OR 97102
Change the Postal Code to 971035	Notice that only the first five numbers, 97103, appear in the field. This occurs because you had set the FieldSize property to five, and 971035 contains six characters.
6 Update the table	

The SmartTags property

Explanation

You can link Access to other applications, such as Outlook, by setting the *SmartTags* property for fields. Smart tags provide certain actions that you can specify for the values in the fields.

To set the SmartTags property for a field:
1 Open the table in Design view.
2 Display the general properties of the field for which you want to assign a smart tag.
3 Click the Smart Tags properties box.
4 Click the Build button next to the Smart Tags property box to open the Smart Tags dialog box, as shown in Exhibit 4-1. The Smart Tags dialog box displays the smart tags that are already installed.
5 Check the relevant smart tag.
6 Click OK to close the Smart Tags dialog box.

After setting a smart tag, you can use it to link the Access database table to other applications, such as Outlook. For example, you can set the smart tag for the name of a person. The smart tag then makes it easier to send e-mail to that person by using Outlook. To do this:
1 Point to the field where you've set the smart tag.
2 Click the smart tag. The Smart Tag Actions menu appears.
3 Choose Send Mail to open a new Message window in Outlook.
4 Specify the details of the message and click Send.

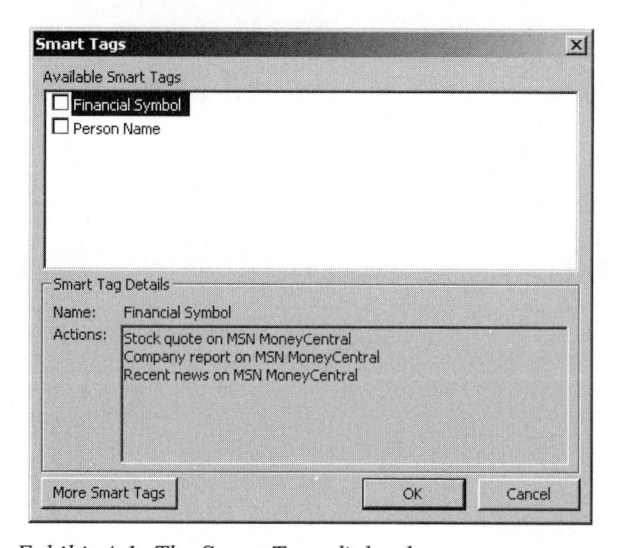

Exhibit 4-1: The Smart Tags dialog box

A-4: Setting the SmartTags property

Here's how	Here's why
1 Switch to Design view	
2 Display the general properties for the field strLastName	
3 On the Field Properties pane, click as shown	Smart Tags
4 Click the Build button next to the Smart Tags property box, as shown	To open the Smart Tags dialog box, shown in Exhibit 4-1.
5 Check **Person name** Click **OK**	(To close the Smart Tags dialog box.) The smart tag you specified appears in the Smart Tags field property box.
6 Update the table	
7 Switch to Datasheet view	A small triangle appears in the corner of the Last Name field. This indicates that you have set the SmartTags property for this field.
8 Point as shown	Last Name / Phone — Murray (2) 665-4500 x123 — Schaaf (624) 390-8944
Click as shown	Last Name / Phone — Murray 665-4500 x123 — Schaaf (624) 390-8944 — Rivet (523) — Smart Tag Actions. To display the Smart Tag Actions menu.
Observe the Smart Tag Actions menu	You can choose any of these actions. For example, to send e-mail to Murray, select Send Mail.
Press (ESC)	To close the menu.

Topic B: Working with input masks

This topic covers the following Microsoft Office Specialist exam objective.

#	Objective
AC03S-1-4	Modifying field properties to display input masks

Input masks

Explanation

An *input mask* defines how data should be entered in a field. The input mask also determines the type of data and the number of characters in it. For example, if you want all phone numbers in a table to contain only numbers and to appear in the same format, you can use an input mask such as (999) 999-9999.

To specify the display format for the data, use the Format property for a field or a control. For example, you can format all dates in the month/day/year format or some other format. You can choose from a list of predefined formats for fields with the AutoNumber, Number, Currency, Date/Time, and Yes/No data types, or you can create your own custom format for any data type except OLE Object. The *OLE Object* data type is used to link to objects created in other applications, such as Microsoft Word.

Creating input masks

An input mask generally consists of literal characters, such as hyphens, underscores, or dashes, which separate blanks. Blanks are used as placeholders for data. Blanks are visible only in Datasheet view. You create an input mask in a field's property sheet by defining the *InputMask property*. For example, for the phone number input mask, you enter digits into the blanks.

An input mask definition contains three sections separated by semicolons:

- The first section contains the input mask. For example, the mask 000-000-0000 specifies that the field should contain 10 numbers and that they should be formatted exactly as shown, separated by hyphens.
- The second section determines whether to store the literal characters that are entered in the field along with the characters that have been entered in the blanks. To define a literal character, enter any character other than the valid input-mask characters, including spaces and symbols. To define one of the valid input-mask characters as a literal character, precede that character with a backslash (\). If you specify 0 in the second section of the input mask, this indicates that you want to store both the literal characters and the values entered in the blanks. If you specify 1 or leave this section blank, this indicates that you want to store only the values entered in the blanks. For example, assume that you specify an input mask for the Phone field, where the first section contains 000-000-0000 and the second section contains 0. If you enter 214-333-4444 as the value in the field, Access will store 214-333-4444 in the field. However, if you specify 1 in the second section, Access will store 2143334444 in the field.
- The third section specifies the characters that will appear as placeholders for the blanks in the input mask. For example, if you specify * as a placeholder for the input mask 000-000-0000, then ***-***-**** appears in the field in the table's Datasheet view.

To create an input mask:
1 Open the table in Design view.
2 Display the general properties for the field that you want to define an input mask for.
3 Click the Input Mask box.
4 Enter the input mask.
5 Update and close the table.

Input-mask characters

You can create input masks by specifying several input-mask characters provided by Access. Access has specific interpretations for each of these characters. To use any of these characters as literal characters, you must precede them with a backslash (\). The following table lists some of the characters you can use when creating input masks:

Character	Description
0	The user must enter a number between 0 and 9.
9	The user can enter a number (0 through 9) or a space, but entry is optional.
#	The user can enter a number or a space. Entry is optional, and all blank positions will be converted to spaces.
L	The user must enter a letter, A through Z.
?	The user can enter a letter, A through Z, but entry is optional.
A	The user must enter either a letter or a number.
a	The user can enter a letter or a number, but entry is optional.
&	The user must enter a character or a space.
C	The user can enter a character or a space, but entry is optional.
<	Any letter that follows will be converted to lowercase.
>	Any letter that follows will be converted to uppercase.
Password	Setting the InputMask property to the word Password creates a password entry text box. Any character typed in the text box is stored as the character but is displayed as an asterisk (*).

Data entry rules **4–11**

Do it! **B-1: Creating an input mask**

Here's how	Here's why
1 Switch to Design view	
2 Display the general properties for the strPhone field	
3 In the Input Mask box, enter **(999) 000-0000;0;#**	To set the Input Mask property. In the first section, the first three blanks contain 9, indicating it is not mandatory to enter values in these blanks. The second section of the input mask contains 0, which indicates that the literal characters will be stored along with the values entered in the blanks. The hash character (#) in the third section is the placeholder for the blanks.
4 Update the table	If a smart tag appears for Property Update Options, ignore it.
5 Switch to Datasheet view	You'll test the input mask by entering sample data in the table.
6 Place the insertion point in the Phone field of the record with the Retailer ID 0016 Observe the cell	(336) 684-4700 (###) ###-#### You'll see that hash characters (#) appear in the cell.
7 Enter **ABC**	Nothing appears in the cell because the characters in the cell should always be numbers.
Enter **5033051478**	Notice that the hash characters (#) are replaced with the numbers you enter.
8 Update the table	

The Input Mask Wizard

Explanation

You can use the Input Mask Wizard to create an input mask based on the built-in input masks in Access. To do so:

1. Open the table in Design view.
2. Display the general properties of the field that you want to set an input mask for. Click the Input Mask box, and click the Build button to display the Input Mask Wizard.
3. From the Input Mask list, select the input mask you want. Click Next.
4. In the Input Mask box, change the input mask, if necessary.
5. From the Placeholder list, select a placeholder, if necessary.
6. Select the relevant option to specify whether you want to store the literal characters with the values entered in the blanks. Click Next.
7. Click Finish to create the input mask.

Do it!

B-2: Working with the Input Mask Wizard

Here's how	Here's why
1 In the Fax field, enter **2143334444**	This field does not contain an input mask.
2 Switch to Design view	
3 Display the general properties for the strFax field	You'll set an input mask for this field.
Click the Input Mask box	The Build button appears.
Click ⋯	(The Build button is next to the Input Mask box.) To display the Input Mask Wizard.
4 In the list, verify that Phone Number is selected	
Click **Next**	To move to the next step of the Input Mask Wizard.
5 In the Try It box, enter **2143334444**	Try It: (214) 333-4444
	The number you entered appears in the input-mask format.
Click **Next**	To move to the next step of the Input Mask Wizard.

6	Select the first option, as shown	⦿ With the symbols in the mask, like this: (264) 316-8517 ○ Without the symbols in the mask, like this: 4442315281
		You'll store both the literal characters and the values entered in the field.
	Click **Next**	To move to the next step of the Input Mask Wizard.
7	Click **Finish**	To close the Input Mask Wizard dialog box and to set the input mask for the field.
	Observe the Input Mask box	Input Mask !(999) 000-0000;0;_
		The input mask contains an exclamation mark (!), which causes the input mask to appear from right to left in the table's Datasheet view. In the first section, the first three blanks contain 9, indicating it is not mandatory to enter values in these blanks. The second section of the input mask contains 0, which indicates that the literal characters will be stored along with the values entered in the blanks. The last section contains an underscore (_), which is the placeholder for the blanks.
8	Update the table	If a smart tag appears for Property Update Options, ignore it.
9	Switch to Datasheet view	To view the data in the input-mask format. Notice that the data in the Fax column now appears in the input-mask format.

Topic C: Setting validation rules

Explanation

If you want a field to contain a certain value as soon as a new record is created, you can set a default value for that field. To validate entered data, you can set validation rules to specify conditions for the type of data, the data format, or the number of characters that can be entered. You can display a customized error message for invalid data by setting the field's validation text.

Setting default values

You set the *DefaultValue property* for a field if you want a default value to be assigned for the field, even if you don't enter any value in the field. In Datasheet view, you can change this default value.

To set a default value:

1 Open the table in Design view.
2 Display the general properties for the field you want to set a default value for.
3 Click in the Default Value box.
4 Enter the default value.
5 Update and close the table.

Do it!

C-1: Setting default values

Here's how	Here's why
1 Switch to Design view	
2 Display the general properties for the strCity field	You'll set the DefaultValue property for this field.
3 In the Default Value box, enter **Portland**	To set Portland as the default value of this field.
4 Update the table	
5 Switch to Datasheet view	The default value Portland appears in the City field in the last row.
6 Close the table	

The Validation Rule property

Explanation

You use a *validation rule* to check data that has been entered into a field. As with an input mask, you can set a format template that the data must match, but with a validation rule, you can also use logical operators to check the data against multiple criteria. For instance, you can set a field to be in date format, and set it to reject dates earlier than the current day. If data entered in a field violates the validation rule, an error message appears and prompts for the correct value. You can set the text of the error message in the Validation Text property. Following are some sample validation rules:

Rule	Description
Like "S???"	The value in the field should have four characters. The first character should always be S.
<>0	The value in the field should not be equal to zero (0).
0 or >100	The value in the field should be 0 or greater than 100.
<#1/1/2003	The date in the field should be earlier than January 1, 2003.

To create a validation rule, display the general properties of the field for which you want to set it, then in the Validation Rule box, enter the validation rule.

C-2: Creating validation rules

Here's how	Here's why
1 Open tblProduct in Design view	
Display the general properties for the strUnit field	You'll set a validation rule for this field.
2 In the Validation Rule box, enter **Like "* oz" Or Like "* lb"**	(To set the Validation Rule property.) In the validation rule, "Like" is used to specify that the strUnit field should be entered in the format of the characters you specify after the word Like. The validation rule specifies that the values you enter in the field should end with either "oz" or "lb."
3 Update the table	A message box appears indicating that this process might take a long time. The message box also asks whether you want the existing data to be tested with the new rule.
Click **Yes**	To save the table's design and to test the existing data against the new validation rule.
4 Switch to Datasheet view	
Navigate to the record with the Product ID 34	You'll try to change the value in the Unit field of this record.
5 Edit the value in the Unit field to read **2.5 kg**	
Press TAB	A message box appears, warning that the data you entered violates the field's validation rule.
Click **OK**	You'll enter the correct unit in this cell.
6 Change the Unit to **1 lb**	
Press TAB	No warning message appears.
7 Update the table	

Data entry rules **4–17**

The Validation Text property

Explanation

When you enter data that violates a field's validation rule, Access displays a message box. You can set the *Validation Text property* to display a customized error message in this message box.

To set validation text for a field, display the general properties of the field. In the Validation Text box, enter the text that you want to display in the message box.

Do it!

C-3: Setting validation text

Here's how	Here's why
1 Switch to Design view	You'll specify the validation text for a validation rule.
2 Display the general properties of the strUnit field	If necessary.
In the Validation Text box, enter **The unit of the values in the Unit field should be oz or lb**	To set the Validation Text property for this field.
3 Update the table	
4 Switch to Datasheet view	You'll test the Validation Text property.
5 Navigate to the record with the Product ID 34	You'll try to change the Unit for this record.
Change the Unit to **2.5 kg**	
Press `TAB`	A message box appears, displaying the validation text that you set.
6 Click **OK**	(To close the message box.) You'll enter the correct unit.
Change the Unit to **1 lb**	
7 Update and close the table	

Topic D: Using indexes

Explanation

You use *indexes* to arrange data in the ascending order of value in a field and to find data in tables. An index performs searches based on key values. Primary key values are automatically indexed, but you can also create indexes based on other values. An index in Access is similar to the index of a book, which you use to locate information. You need to create indexes on only those fields that you frequently search, sort, or join. There are two types of indexes: single-field and multiple-field.

Single-field indexes

A *single-field index* is based on one field in a table. This index helps you find and sort data in tables that contain large amounts of data. For example, you can create a single-field index for Order Date in the tblOrder table to sort and find data based on order dates.

To create a single-field index:

1. In Design view, open the table for which you want to create an index.
2. Choose View, Indexes to open the Indexes window.
3. Under Index Name, click the relevant cell.
4. Enter the name of the index, and press Tab.
5. From the list, select the field on which you want to create the index. Press Tab.
6. Select the sort order, and close the window.

You can also create a single-field index by selecting a field and setting the Indexed property to Yes.

Do it!

D-1: Creating a single-field index

Here's how	Here's why
1 Open tblRetailer in Design view	You'll add an index to the table.
2 Choose **View**, **Indexes**	(To display the Indexes: tblRetailer window.) tblRetailer is indexed on the primary key lngRetailerID.
3 Under Index Name, click the second cell	
4 Enter **RetailerName** Press `TAB`	To enter the name of the new index.
5 From the list, select **strRetailerName**	To select the field that you want to base the index on.
6 Under Sort Order, in the third cell, verify that Ascending appears	
7 Close the window	

Multiple-field indexes

Explanation

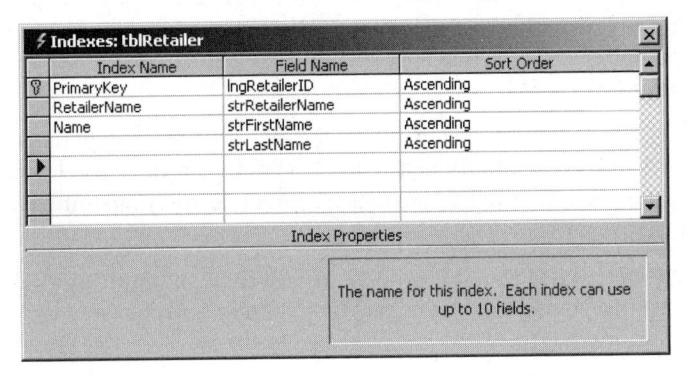

You can create a *multiple-field* index based on two or more fields in a table. For example, you can create an index based on the First Name and Last Name fields in the tblRetailer table. To do so, click the Indexes button on the Table Design toolbar to open the Indexes<table name> window, where <table name> represents the name of the table. Select the fields on which you want to base the index, and then close the window.

Index Name	Field Name	Sort Order
PrimaryKey	lngRetailerID	Ascending
RetailerName	strRetailerName	Ascending
Name	strFirstName	Ascending
	strLastName	Ascending

Indexes: tblRetailer

Index Properties: The name for this index. Each index can use up to 10 fields.

Exhibit 4-2: The Indexes window

Do it!

D-2: Creating a multiple-field index

Here's how	Here's why
1 Click [icon]	(On the Table Design toolbar.) To open the Indexes: tblRetailer window.
2 Under Index Name, click the third cell	You'll create a multiple-field index.
3 Enter **Name**	
Press (TAB)	You'll select the field that you want to base the index on.
4 From the list, select **strFirstName**	
5 Under Field Name, click the fourth cell	You'll select another field for the index.
6 From the list, select **strLastName**	
7 Under Sort Order, in the third and fourth cells, verify that Ascending appears	The window will look like Exhibit 4-2
8 Close the window	
9 Update and close the table	
10 Close the database	

Unit summary: Data entry rules

Topic A In this topic, you learned how to set the Required, AllowZeroLength, FieldSize, and SmartTags properties for a field. You learned that by setting these **field properties**, you could control how data is displayed and stored in a table.

Topic B In this topic, you learned how to set **input masks** for a field in a table by entering the input mask in a field's property sheet. You learned that an input mask specifies the format for entering data in a field. You also learned how to set the input mask by using the **Input Mask Wizard**.

Topic C In this topic, you learned how to set the **DefaultValue** property for a field. You also created and set a **validation rule** for a field. In addition, you learned how to set validation text for a field. You learned how to display **customized messages** by setting validation text.

Topic D In this topic, you learned how to set **single-field** and **multiple-field indexes**. You learned that setting indexes helps you **perform searches** in a table.

Independent practice activity

1. Open DefiningDataEntryRules.
2. Set the Required property for the strProductName field of the tblProduct table to Yes.
3. Update and close the table.
4. Create an input mask for the strPhone field in the tblRetailer table. Edit the input mask to read **000\-000\-0000;1;***. This will ensure that only 10 numbers are entered in the field, and although the input mask will display numbers in a specific format in the table, only the numbers (not the literal characters) are stored in the table. Use an asterisk (*) as a placeholder.000\-000\-0000;1;*
5. Update the table.
6. Test the input mask by entering sample data.
7. Close the table.
8. Set the DefaultValue property for the curUnitPrice field of the tblProduct table to 0.00.
9. Update and close the table.
10. Create a validation rule for the dtmOrderDate field in the tblOrder table to ensure that the dates entered are after 1/1/2003. (*Hint:* Enter the validation rule **>#1/1/2003#** in the Validation Rule box.) Set validation text for the rule.
11. Update the table.
12. Test the validation rule by entering sample data.
13. Close the table.
14. Create a single-field index based on the field name lngItemOrdID in the tblOrderItem table.
15. Update and close the table.
16. Close the database.

Review questions

1 Which field property is used to specify that the field can contain null values?

   A Required

   B AllowZeroLength

   C FieldSize

   D Format

2 Which field property is used to specify actions, such as sending e-mail, for the data values in the fields?

   A Required

   B AllowZeroLength

   C FieldSize

   D SmartTags

3 Which field property is used to guarantee that the field is not left blank?

   A Required

   B AllowZeroLength

   C FieldSize

   D Format

4 What is the definition of a null value?

5 Describe the three sections of an input mask.

6 When creating an input mask, how do you indicate literal characters?

7 Identify the correct character for each of the following:

Description	Character
The user must enter a number between 0 and 9.	
The user can enter a number (0 through 9) or a space, but entry is optional.	
The users must enter a letter, A through Z.	
The user can enter a letter (A through Z), but entry is optional.	
The user can enter a number or a space. Entry is optional, and all blank positions will be converted to spaces.	

8 Which field property is used to display a customized error message?

A Default Value

B Validation Test

C Validation Text

D Field Message Text

Unit 5
Simple queries

Unit time: 50 minutes

Complete this unit, and you'll know how to:

A Plan, create, save, and run queries; and use queries to sort data and to filter query results.

B Modify queries and query results by adding and removing fields; and find records with empty fields.

C Perform operations in queries by using comparison operators; use AND and OR conditions in queries; and use expressions and aggregate functions.

Topic A: Creating and using queries

This topic covers the following Microsoft Office Specialist exam objectives.

#	Objective
AC03S-1-7	Creating and modifying Select queries using the Simple Query Wizard
AC03S-3-5	Sorting records in tables, queries, forms and reports (This objective is also covered in the units titled "Fields and records," "Using forms," and "Working with reports.")

Using queries to retrieve data

Explanation

A *query* is a database object that retrieves and displays selective data from one or more tables. You can use a query to retrieve data meeting specific conditions from specific fields. For example, if you want to see all the products with a unit price greater than $2, you can specify this condition in a query.

When a query is executed, the results are displayed in Datasheet view. The format of each field that appears in a query datasheet (the result) depends on the properties set in the base table. You can edit, navigate, sort, and filter these results just as you would do in a table in Datasheet view. A *filter* is a set of conditions applied to data to view a section of data. Query results are similar to the results of a filter, but a query is a database object that you can save permanently, whereas a filter provides only a temporary view.

To extract data by using a query, you need to plan and define the following:

- The conditions that you want the data to meet
- The fields that you want to see in the query result
- The tables from which you'll extract the fields
- The statements that you'll use to extract data

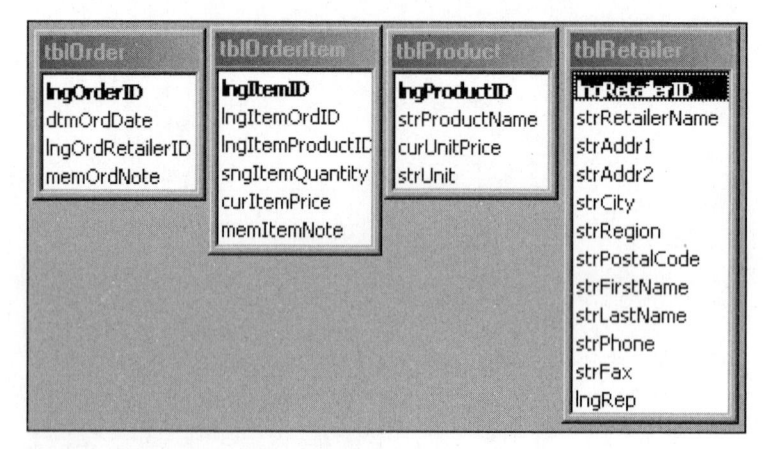

Exhibit 5-1: The tables in a database

Do it!

A-1: Planning a query

Questions and answers

1. You have designed a database containing the tables as shown in Exhibit 5-1. With respect to these tables, answer the following:

    You need to extract product details for all records with a unit price greater than $3. On what field would the condition apply?

    You want to display the details of the retailers in a specific city that is in a specific region. On what fields would this condition apply, and from which table would you extract this information?

    What fields would you want to display when you run the query to display records with a unit price greater than $3?

    From which table would you extract the information?

Simple queries

Explanation

A simple query can retrieve data from fields in one or more tables or queries. You can use the Simple Query Wizard to create a simple query:

1. On the Objects bar, click Queries to start working with a query object.
2. Click the New button on the Database window toolbar to open the New Query dialog box.
3. From the dialog box, select Simple Query Wizard and click OK to open the first dialog box of the Simple Query Wizard, as shown in Exhibit 5-2.
4. From the Tables/Queries list, select the table that you want to base the query on.
5. From the Available Fields list, select the fields for the query, and add them to the Selected Fields list. Click Next to move to the next dialog box.
6. Select the relevant option to display either detailed results or a summary of the query result. This dialog box will appear only if you select a numeric field for your query. Click Next. In the What title do you want for your query? box, specify a title for the query.
7. Select the option to either open the query or modify its design. Click Finish to exit the wizard and create the query.

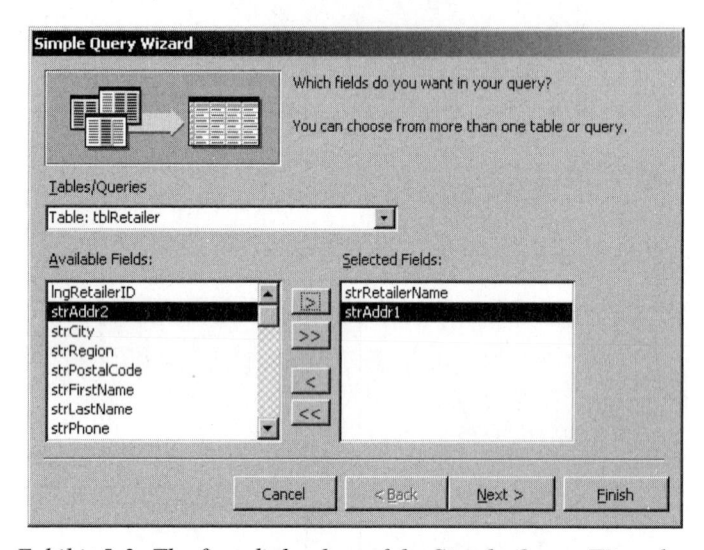

Exhibit 5-2: The first dialog box of the Simple Query Wizard

Do it!

A-2: Using the Simple Query Wizard

Here's how	Here's why
1 Open the database CreateQuery	(From the current unit folder.) You'll create a query to view the names and addresses of the retailers from the tblRetailer table.
2 On the Objects bar, click **Queries**	
3 Click **New**	(The New button is on the Database window toolbar.) To open the New Query dialog box.

Simple queries 5–5

4	From the dialog box, select **Simple Query Wizard**	You'll create a query by using the wizard.
	Click **OK**	To open the Simple Query Wizard.
5	From the Tables/Queries list, select **Table: tblRetailer**	(You'll create the query based on this table.) The fields of the selected table, tblRetailer, appear in the Available Fields list, as shown in Exhibit 5-2.
6	From the Available Fields list, select **strRetailerName**	
	Click `>`	(The Add button is on the Simple Query Wizard.) To add the field to the Selected Fields list.
	Add **strAddr1** to the Selected Fields list	Select the field from the Available Fields list, and click the Add button.
	Click **Next**	To move to the next step of the wizard.
7	Edit the What title do you want for your query? box to read **qryRetailerDetails**	This will be the title of the query.
	Verify that the first option is selected, as shown	
		You'll view the query results as soon as you finish creating the query.
	Click **Finish**	To view the query results in Datasheet view.
8	Observe the result	
		The retailers' names and addresses appear in the query result. By default, the record selector is on the first record.
9	Close the query	(Choose File, Close.) The qryRetailerDetails query appears in the Database window.

Creating queries in Design view

Explanation

You can use a query Design view to create or modify queries. For simple queries, Design view contains a design grid in its lower pane, as shown in Exhibit 5-3. In its upper pane, Design view contains the field list for the table or tables on which the query is based. A field list displays all the fields in the record source. To create a query, you must select one or more data sources and define the specifications of the query in Design view. The source for the queries can be other queries or tables.

To create a simple query in Design view:

1. Open the database.
2. On the Objects bar, click Queries to start working with a query object.
3. Click the New button on the Database window toolbar to open the New Query dialog box.
4. In the dialog box, verify that Design View is selected, and click OK to open the Show Table dialog box.
5. In the dialog box, select the table you want to add to the query, and click Add. Then click Close to return to Design view.
6. Select the fields that you want to display in the query result.

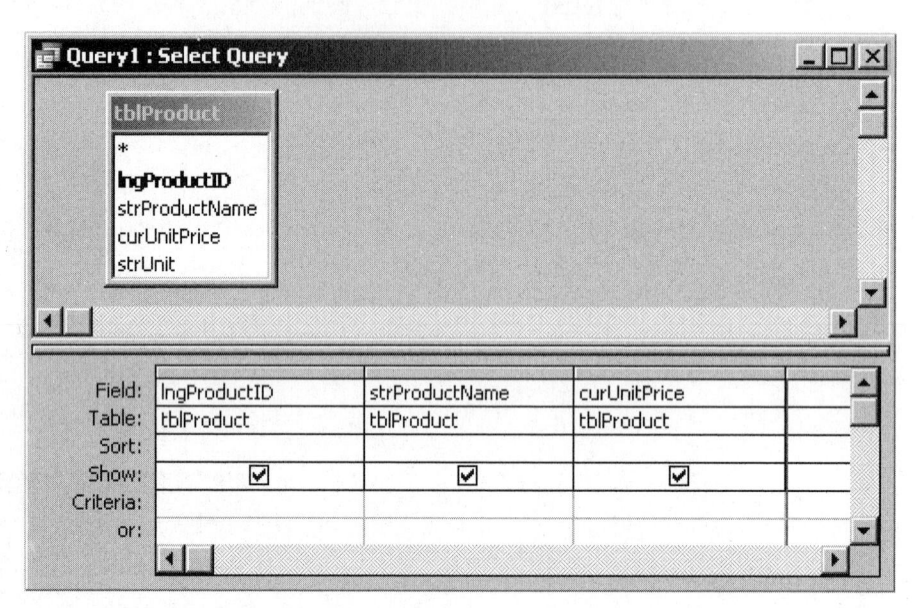

Exhibit 5-3: Creating a query in Design view

Do it!

A-3: Creating a query in Design view

Here's how	Here's why
1 On the Objects bar, verify that Queries is selected	You'll create a query to view three selected fields from the tblProduct table.
2 Click **New**	(The New button is on the Database window toolbar.) To open the New Query dialog box.
3 Verify that Design View is selected	You'll create the query in Design view.
4 Click **OK**	To open the Show Table dialog box.
5 Verify that the Tables tab is activated	A list of tables appears.
6 Select **tblProduct**	The query will be based on this table.
Click **Add**	To add the table to the upper pane in Design view.
Click **Close**	To close the Show Table dialog box.
7 Observe Design view	The upper pane displays the field list for the tblProduct table.
In the lower pane of the design grid, verify that the insertion point is in the first cell of the Field row	You'll enter a field here.
8 Display the field list in the first cell of the Field row	tblProduct.* lngProductID strProductName curUnitPrice strUnit The field list contains the table name with an asterisk (*) and the names of all the fields in the table.
9 From the list, select **lngProductID**	To add this field to the design grid.
Observe the design grid	Field: lngProductID Table: tblProduct Sort: Show: ☑ Criteria: or: The design grid displays lngProductID in the first cell of the Field row. tblProduct appears in the Table row, and the check box in the Show row is checked. This indicates that the field lngProductID will appear in the query result.

10	Place the insertion point in the second cell of the Field row	You'll select the second field from the list.
	From the list, select **strProductName**	To add strProductName to the design grid.
11	Add curUnitPrice to the design grid	From the list in the third cell of the Field row, select curUnitPrice.
	Observe the design grid	The design grid displays the fields lngProductID, strProductName, and curUnitPrice, as shown in Exhibit 5-3. These three fields will appear in the query result.

Saving and viewing query results

Explanation

You can save a query in several ways: by choosing File, Save As; by clicking the Save button on the Query Design toolbar; or by choosing File, Save. When you choose File, Save As, the Save As dialog box appears. You can then specify the name of the query in the Save Query 'Query1' To box, and click OK.

To see the results of the query, you must run it. To run the query, choose Query, Run in Design view. You can also select the query in the Database window and click Open on the Database window toolbar, or click the Run button on the Query Design toolbar.

Exhibit 5-4: The query result that appears after Step 3 of the activity

Do it!

A-4: Saving and running the query

Here's how	Here's why
1 Choose **File, Save As...**	To open the Save As dialog box.
2 Edit the Save Query 'Query1' To box to read **qrySimpleQuery**	To name the query qrySimpleQuery.
Verify that Query appears in the As list	
Click **OK**	(To save the query with the specified name.) The title bar of the Design window displays the name qrySimpleQuery: Select Query.
3 Choose **Query, Run**	(To run the query.) The qrySimpleQuery : Select Query window appears, as shown in Exhibit 5-4. The fields Product ID, Product Name, and Unit Price appear in Datasheet view. The record selector is on the first record.

Sorting query results in Design view

Explanation

Sorting refers to organizing records either in ascending order or in descending order based on the contents of a field. You can sort query results in the same way that you sort records in a table. The sort order is evaluated from left to right. The left sort field is the primary sort field. You can save the sort order with the query object. If you do not specify any sort order, the records are sorted by the primary key field of the table.

To sort records in a query:

1 In the design grid, place the insertion point in the preferred cell of the Sort row. A drop-down arrow appears in the right corner of the cell.
2 Display the Sort list, and select a sort order.
3 Run the query.

Do it!

A-5: Sorting query results

Here's how	Here's why
1 Click	(The View button is on the Query Datasheet toolbar.) To switch to Design view.
2 Place the insertion point in the third cell of the Sort row	(Under curUnitPrice.) To sort the records based on the field curUnitPrice.
3 Display the Sort list, as shown	
4 Select **Descending**	(To arrange the records in descending order of curUnitPrice.) In the third cell of the Sort row, Descending is selected.
5 Click	(The Run button is on the Query Design toolbar.) To run the query.
Observe the results	

Product ID	Product Name	Unit Price
34	Chives (Bulk)	$17.00
33	Cinnamon Ground (Bulk)	$14.89
29	Carob Pods	$12.49
12	De Arbol Peppers (Whole)	$5.50
11	De Arbol Pepper (Ground)	$4.25
7	Chinese Star Anise (Ground)	$3.50
1	Cassia	$3.00
2	Catnip Leaf	$2.75
32	Caraway Seed	$2.50
24	Cinnamon Ground	$2.29
6	Chili Pepper Powder	$2.00
10	Cilantro Flakes	$2.00
25	Cinnamon (Ground) Extra High Oil (2	$1.99

The records in the query results are sorted based on the descending order of the values in the Unit Price field.

6 Switch to Design view — You'll continue working in Design view.

Specifying criteria to filter queries

Explanation

You can filter records by specifying criteria. You use criteria to specify a condition in the design grid to display specific records. For example, you can specify criteria to view the products sold on a specific date, or view the products whose unit price is greater than a specific value, or view the records that contain a specific value for a specific field. To add a criterion to a query, specify the criterion in the Criteria row, and run the query.

Do it!

A-6: Filtering query results

Here's how	Here's why
1 Place the insertion point in the first cell of the Criteria row	You'll specify a query criterion for the field lngProductID.
2 Enter **3**	This query criterion will display details about the product with Product ID 3 in the query result.
3 Run the query	Click the Run button on the Query Design toolbar.
Observe the query result	It shows the Product Name and Unit Price for Product ID 3.

Topic B: Modifying query results and queries

Explanation

After you've run a query and got the results, you might need to change values in the source table. For example, if the address of a retailer changes and you want to reflect this change in the query, you can do this by modifying the data in the query result, which will, in turn, modify the data in the source table.

After you've created a query, you might need to modify it. You can do this by adding or deleting fields in Design view.

If table records contain fields where no data has been entered, you can find those records by using Is Null as the criterion in the design grid of the query. A field is null when it does not contain a value.

Editing query results in Datasheet view

If you make any changes in the records shown in the query result, the same changes are reflected in the table on which the query is based. To edit a record in a query result, you enter the new values in Datasheet view and save the query result. You can then open the source table to view the edited values.

Do it!

B-1: Editing query results

Here's how	Here's why
1 In the record, change Unit Price to **2.35**	(To edit a value in the query result in Datasheet view.) This will be the new value for the Unit Price of the product with the Product ID 3.
Update the query result	(Choose File, Save.) To update the table on which the query is based.
2 Close the query	Choose File, Close.
3 On the Objects bar, click **Tables**	
4 Open **tblProduct**	You'll check whether the value you changed in the query result is reflected in the tblProduct table.
Observe the record with the Product ID 3	The Unit Price for the product with the Product ID 3 is now $2.35. The value modified in the query result is reflected in the source table.
5 Close the table	

Simple queries 5–13

Modifying the query design

Explanation To edit a query, first open it in Design view. From the field list, select the fields you want to add. Then, run the query to view the updated result.

Do it! **B-2: Adding fields to a query**

Here's how	Here's why
1 On the Objects bar, click **Queries**	
2 Select **qrySimpleQuery**	If necessary.
Click **Design**	(The Design button is on the Database window toolbar.) To open qrySimpleQuery in Design view. You'll modify your earlier query by adding the field strUnit to it.
Delete 3 from the Criteria row	To delete the criteria set to display only details about the product with Product ID 3.
3 Place the insertion point in the fourth cell of the Field row	You'll add another field to the query.
4 From the field list, select **strUnit**	To add this field to the query.
5 Run the query	The query result now contains one additional field, Unit.

Removing fields

Explanation To remove a field from the query, select the entire column in the design grid and delete the column. You can also choose Edit, Delete Columns to delete a selected column.

Do it! **B-3: Removing fields from a query**

Here's how	Here's why
1 Switch to Design view	Click the View button on the Query Datasheet toolbar.
2 Click above the Field row in the strProductName column, as shown	![strProductName/tblProduct column selection] (To select the column.) You'll remove this field from the query.
3 Choose **Edit, Delete Columns**	To delete this column from the query.
4 Run the query	The field Product Name no longer appears.

Records with empty fields

Explanation

An empty field sometimes causes problems in a table. For example, if you want to multiply values in the fields Quantity and Price Paid, and if one of these fields does not contain a value, you'll get an incorrect result. You might want to display or remove fields that don't contain values. Unknown (empty) values in fields are referred to as *null* values. Null values cannot be entered in the primary key field, nor can they be used in calculations. You can specify Is Null in the field criteria to find all records where no entry has been made in a specific field.

To search for records that contain null values, enter Is Null in the specific cell in the Criteria row, and run the query.

Do it!

B-4: Finding records with empty fields

Here's how	Here's why
1 Switch to Design view	
2 Place the insertion point in the third cell of the Criteria row	(Under strUnit.) You'll search for records that do not have any values in the strUnit field.
3 Enter **Is Null**	This criterion ensures that the records with null values in the strUnit field appear in the query result.
4 Run the query		Product ID	Unit Price	Unit	| ▶ | 27 | $1.49 | | A record with an empty Unit field appears.

Topic C: Performing operations in queries

This topic covers the following Microsoft Office Specialist exam objectives.

#	Objective
AC03S-3-1	Adding calculated fields to queries in Query Design view (This objective is also covered in *Access 2003: Intermediate*, in the unit titled "Complex queries.")
AC03S-3-1	Using aggregate functions in queries (e.g., AVG, COUNT) (This objective is also covered in *Access 2003: Intermediate*, in the unit titled "Complex queries.")

Explanation

You can perform comparison operations or calculations by using queries. If you want to view records based on multiple conditions, you can add criteria to a query by using the comparison operators. To create a query containing multiple criteria, you can use the AND condition or the OR condition. You can also add a specific criterion in the query for a text field by using a wildcard operator.

Sometimes you might need to perform calculations on existing field values. For example, based on the values of the field Unit Price in the tblProduct table, you might want to calculate discounts for each product. If you want to calculate values based on the fields in a table, you don't need to add a new field to the table to store the calculated values. Instead, you can use a query object to create a calculated field from the data in the source table. Using a query object ensures that the calculated field always contains the latest value, and the table takes up less space in computer memory because the calculated values are not stored in the source table. Calculations are performed each time the query is run. To perform calculations on a group of records, you can use aggregate functions, such as Sum, Avg, Count, or Min, in Design view.

Comparison operators

You use a comparison operator in a query to find records with matching values in one or more fields. A comparison operator is a symbol such as > (greater than) or < (less than). For example, you can search for all records with a unit price greater than (>) 2.35.

You can also use comparison operators to specify a condition for a query. To use a comparison operator, place the insertion point in the proper cell of the Criteria row. Enter the criteria by using a comparison operator, and run the query.

The following table lists the comparison operators:

Operator	Description
>	Greater than
<	Less than
=	Equal to
<=	Less than or equal to
>=	Greater than or equal to
<>	Not equal to

Do it! **C-1: Using comparison operators**

Here's how	Here's why
1 Switch to Design view	
2 Delete the previous criterion	(Select Is Null, and press Delete.) You'll edit this query to specify a criterion using a comparison operator.
3 Place the insertion point in the second cell of the Criteria row	
4 Enter **>2.3**	To enter a query for viewing the details of products whose Unit Price is greater than $2.30.
5 Run the query	

Product ID	Unit Price	Unit
34	$17.00	1 lb
33	$14.89	1 lb
29	$12.49	6 oz
12	$5.50	2 oz
11	$4.25	2 oz
7	$3.50	0.5 oz
1	$3.00	2 oz
2	$2.75	2.25 oz
32	$2.50	2.5 oz
3	$2.35	2.35 oz

The records with a Unit Price greater than $2.30 appear in the result.

OR conditions

Explanation

You might want to specify two conditions in the criteria and display the records that satisfy either of these conditions. For example, you might want to see records whose unit price is greater than $2 or whose unit is equal to 2 oz. To display these records, you can use an OR condition for specifying the criteria.

To filter query results with the OR condition, enter the condition in the proper cell(s) of the row in the design grid, and run the query.

Do it!

C-2: Using the OR condition

Here's how	Here's why
1 Switch to Design view	
2 Delete the previous criterion	
3 Place the insertion point in the second cell of the Criteria row	(If necessary.) You will enter a criterion for the field curUnitPrice.
4 Enter **>2.0**	You want to find records with a Unit Price greater than $2.00.
5 Place the insertion point in the third cell of the Or row	Under strUnit.
6 Enter **>1.5 oz**	This will be the criterion for strUnit.
7 Run the query	*[Table showing:]* Product ID / Unit Price / Unit 34 / $17.00 / 1 lb 33 / $14.89 / 1 lb 29 / $12.49 / 6 oz 12 / $5.50 / 2 oz 11 / $4.25 / 2 oz 7 / $3.50 / 0.5 oz 1 / $3.00 / 2 oz 2 / $2.75 / 2.25 oz 32 / $2.50 / 2.5 oz 3 / $2.35 / 2.35 oz 24 / $2.29 / 2 oz 6 / $2.00 / 2.25 oz 10 / $2.00 / 2.75 oz Products appear that have either a unit price greater than $2.00 or a unit greater than 1.5 oz, or both.

AND conditions

Explanation

When you use more than one condition in a query, you might want the query result to show the records that satisfy all the conditions. For example, you can search for products with a unit price greater than $1.40 and less than $1.90. Here, you can use the AND condition. The query result will show only the records that satisfy both conditions.

To use an AND condition, enter the AND condition in the proper cell of the Criteria row, and run the query.

Do it!

C-3: Using the AND condition

Here's how	Here's why
1 Switch to Design view	
2 Delete both the previous criteria	
3 Place the insertion point in the second cell of the Criteria row	(If necessary.) You'll enter a criterion for curUnitPrice.
4 Enter **>1.4And<1.9**	
5 Run the query	*[Table showing:]* Product ID | Unit Price | Unit 30 | $1.89 | 1.5 oz 28 | $1.89 | 3 oz 4 | $1.50 | 1 oz 27 | $1.49 | 26 | $1.49 | 0.5 oz 31 | $1.45 | 2 oz The results show those products that have a unit price greater than 1.4 and less than 1.9.

Wildcard operators

Explanation

Wildcard operators are used to retrieve multiple values. You might not be able to remember the exact text when you're specifying text values as a criterion. In such cases, you can use a wildcard operator to specify criteria. For example, if you can remember only the first letter of the text you want to search for, you can use a wildcard. *Wildcards* are operators that you can use as placeholders.

There are two frequently used wildcard operators: the question mark (?) and the asterisk (*). The question mark is used to substitute for a single character. The asterisk is used to substitute for any number of characters.

For example, you can use A* to search for product names beginning with the letter A. When you run the query, Access inserts a Like operator and surrounds the character and the * with double quotation marks. A Like operator is used to search for specific text. In the previous example, the Like operator searches for text like A* where the asterisk can represent any character or characters.

To use a wildcard operator, enter the wildcard in the proper cell of the Criteria row, and run the query.

Do it!

C-4: Using the * wildcard

Here's how	Here's why
1 Switch to Design view	
2 Delete the previous criterion	
3 Add the field strProductName to the design grid	Place the insertion point in the fourth cell of the Field row, and select strProductName from the field list.
4 Place the insertion point in the fourth cell of the Criteria row	(Under strProductName.) You'll use a wildcard operator.
5 Enter **A***	To search for all products whose name starts with A.
Press `TAB`	To move to the next cell. The criteria under strProductName changes to Like "A*".
6 Run the query	

Product ID	Unit Price	Unit	Product Name
27	$1.49		Anise Seeds
26	$1.49	0.5 oz	Asafoetida Powder
23	$1.23	1.5 oz	Annatto Seed

The results show product details for product names beginning with A.

Using calculations

Explanation

When creating a calculated field, you must enclose field names referenced in an expression in square brackets. An *expression* is a combination of symbols—identifiers, operators, and values—that produces a result. An expression can include the normal arithmetic operators for addition (+), subtraction (-), multiplication (*), and division (/).

To use calculations in a query, enter the expression in the proper cell of the Field row, and run the query.

Product ID	Unit Price	Unit	Product Name	Discount
34	$17.00	1 lb	Chives (Bulk)	1.7
33	$14.89	1 lb	Cinnamon Ground (Bulk)	1.489
29	$12.49	6 oz	Carob Pods	1.249
12	$5.50	2 oz	De Arbol Peppers (Whole)	0.55
11	$4.25	2 oz	De Arbol Pepper (Ground)	0.425
7	$3.50	0.5 oz	Chinese Star Anise (Ground)	0.35
1	$3.00	2 oz	Cassia	0.3
2	$2.75	2.25 oz	Catnip Leaf	0.275
32	$2.50	2.5 oz	Caraway Seed	0.25
3	$2.35	2.35 oz	Celery Seed (Whole)	0.235
24	$2.29	2 oz	Cinnamon Ground	0.229

Exhibit 5-5: The query result containing the calculated field that appears after Step 5 of the activity

Do it!

C-5: Using calculations in a query

Here's how	Here's why
1 Switch to Design view	
2 Delete the previous criterion	
3 Place the insertion point in the fifth cell of the Field row	To enter an expression to calculate a discount.
4 Enter **Discount:[curUnitPrice]*0.1**	
	To calculate the discount as 10% of the Unit Price. Here, the calculated field is Discount.
5 Run the query	(The results appear, as shown in Exhibit 5-5.) A new field, Discount, appears in the table. This field contains the calculated discount values.
6 Update and close the query	

Calculating totals

Explanation

You might need to perform calculations on groups of records instead of on single records. For example, while viewing a set of records containing information about products sold in each order, you might also want to view the total sales of these same products. To calculate values for a group of records, you can use *aggregate functions* by adding the values to the Total row of the query design grid. The Total row appears in the design grid when you click the Totals button on the Query Design toolbar.

You use the Sum aggregate function to total the values for a field. The Max and Min aggregate functions are used to find the maximum and minimum values of a field. You can use the Group By calculation to group records based on similar field values.

Do it!

C-6: Totaling a group of records

Here's how	Here's why
1 Open the tblOrderItem table	(On the Objects bar, click Tables; double-click the table.) You'll determine the total of price paid in each order. Several records contain the same value for Order ID. You can create a query to total the values in the field Price Paid grouped by Order ID.
Close the window	
2 On the Objects bar, click **Queries**	
3 Create a new query in Design view	(On the Database window toolbar, click New; verify that Design View is selected; then click OK.) You'll use the new query to total the values in the field curItemPrice grouped by lngItemOrdID.
4 Add tblOrderItem to the query	In the Show Table dialog box, select tblOrderItem, click Add, and then click Close.
5 Add the fields lngItemOrdID and curItemPrice to the Field row	
6 Click Σ	(The Totals button is on the Query Design toolbar.) The Total row appears. In the Total row, Group By appears.
Place the insertion point in the second cell of the Total row	
7 Display the Total list	

8 From the list, select **Sum** To calculate the sum of the values in the field curItemPrice.

9 Run the query

Order ID	SumOfcurItemPrice
1	$12.75
2	$5.25
3	$1.00
4	$23.39
5	$4.23
6	$16.39

The heading Price Paid changes to SumOfcurItemPrice. Under this heading, the sum of the price paid in each order appears.

10 Switch to Design view

11 Save the query as **qryTotals**

12 Close the query

Access 2003: Basic

The Avg and Count functions

Explanation

You use the Avg aggregate function to find the average of the values in a field for a group of records. For example, you can calculate the average sales of each product.

To find the number of values in a field, you use the Count aggregate function. For example, you can find out the number of products having the same unit price. The Count function does not count fields with null (blank) values.

Do it!

C-7: Using the Avg and Count functions

Here's how	Here's why
1 Create a new query in Design view	You'll create a query to find the average sales of each product.
2 Add tblOrderItem to the query	Add the table, and close the Show Table dialog box.
3 Add the fields lngItemProductID and sngItemQuantity to the Field row	
4 Choose **View**, **Totals**	To add the Total row to the design grid.
5 Display the Total list under the field sngItemQuantity	Click the drop-down arrow next to Group By under sngItemQuantity.
From the list, select **Avg**	You'll calculate the average quantity sold for each product.
6 Run the query	The average quantity sold for each product appears under the heading AvgOfsngItemQuantity.
7 Switch to Design view	
8 Place the insertion point in the first cell of the Total row	(Under lngItemProductID.) You'll now find the number of products sold in each order.
From the Total list, select **Count**	To calculate the total number of values in the field lngItemProductID.
9 Place the insertion point in the second cell of the Field row	
From the field list, select **lngItemOrdID**	You'll find the number of products sold in each order.

10	Under lngItemOrdID, from the Total list, select **Group By**	This will group the records with the same Order ID.
11	Run the query	The number of products sold for each order appears under the heading CountOflngItemProductID.
12	Switch to Design view	
13	Save the query as **qryCalculations**	
14	Close the query and the database	

Unit summary: Simple queries

Topic A In this topic, you learned how to plan and create a **query**. You also created a query by using the **Simple Query Wizard** and Design view. You saved and ran a query. You also learned that you could view query results by running a query. You **sorted** and **filtered** records in the query datasheet.

Topic B In this topic, you learned how to **modify values** in the query result. You changed the values in the source table by modifying the values in the query result. You also **added** and **removed** fields in query Design view. You modified a query by adding and removing fields. You also learned how to use Is Null in the Criteria row to locate null values in a table.

Topic C In this topic, you used **comparison operators** and separated multiple queries on a field by using the **AND** and **OR** conditions. You also used the **asterisk (*) wildcard operator** to view specific text values. You added a **calculated field** to a query by using an **expression**. You also learned how to use **aggregate functions** to perform calculations on groups of records.

Independent practice activity

1. Open Orders.
2. In Design view, create a query, based on the tblOrderItem table, that displays Order ID, Product, and Quantity. Run the query.
3. In Datasheet view, modify the query result by changing the value of Quantity of product with Product ID 5 to 300.
4. Save the query as **qryPractice**.
5. Verify that the change is reflected in the tblOrderItem table.
6. Add a new field, curItemPrice, to the query qryPractice, and run the query.
7. Update and close the query.
8. Create a new query based on the tblProduct table that displays all the products having a Unit Price between $1.00 and $2. Run the query, and compare your results with Exhibit 5-6.
9. Delete the previous criteria, and display all the records where the Product Name begins with **Ce**. Close the query without saving it.
10. Create a new query based on the tblOrder table that displays the count of retailers having orders on the same date. (*Hint:* Use Count in the Total row for the field lngOrdRetailerID, and use Group By in the Total row for the field dtmOrddate.) Compare your results with Exhibit 5-7.
11. Close the query without saving.
12. Close the database.

Product Name	Unit Price
Celery Seed (Whole)	$1.75
Celery Seed (Ground)	$1.50
Chives	$1.25
Annatto Seed	$1.23
Cinnamon (Ground) Extra High Oil (2	$1.99
Asafoetida Powder	$1.49
Anise Seeds	$1.49
Basil Leaf (Whole)	$1.89
Carob Powder (Raw)	$1.89
Basil Leaf (Ground)	$1.45

Exhibit 5-6: The query result after Step 7 of the Independent Practice Activity

CountOfIngOrdRetailerID	Order Date
2	1/6/2004
1	1/8/2004
3	2/2/2004
1	2/9/2004
1	3/1/2004
2	3/6/2004
1	4/1/2004
1	5/6/2004
1	5/21/2004
1	6/11/2004
1	6/23/2004
1	7/7/2004
1	8/9/2004
1	8/11/2004
1	9/9/2004
1	9/22/2004
1	10/12/2004
1	11/1/2004

Exhibit 5-7: The query result after Step 9 of the Independent Practice Activity

Review questions

1 What is a query?

2 If both queries and filters display data based on selection criteria, how are queries and filters different?

3 When using the Simple Query Wizard, what information do you need to provide?

4 Which of the following methods cannot be used to run a query?

   A Choose Query, Run in Design view.

   B Choose Query, Run in the Database window.

   C In the Database window, select the query and click Open.

   D In the Database window, select the query and click Run.

5 In which view do you sort a query?

6 Which field criteria is used to find records where no entry has been made in the specific field?

7 Complete the table by filling in the correct comparison operator for the described query.

Description	Operator
Used to specify more than one condition where the query results need to match only one of the conditions	
Used to specify more than one condition where the query results must match all of the conditions	
Used as a placeholder when specifying criteria	

Unit 6
Using forms

Unit time: 50 minutes

Complete this unit, and you'll know how to:

A Create forms by using the AutoForm feature, use the navigation bar, and enter data into forms.

B Create forms by using the Form Wizard.

C Create and modify forms in Design view.

D Find, sort, and filter records by using forms.

Topic A: Creating forms

This topic covers the following Microsoft Office Specialist exam objective.

#	Objective
AC03S-1-8	Creating AutoForms

Forms

Explanation

A *form* is an Access database object that allows you to view, edit, and add data to a table. Whereas the datasheet view of a table shows you a grid of fields and rows, a form typically shows just one record at a time. The fields can be arranged on a form and labeled for clarity, and they can be made to look like familiar paper documents, such as invoices. In the example shown in Exhibit 6-1, names and addresses are arranged in a familiar format. The underlying table, from which the field values come, is referred to as the *source table*. Well-designed forms make a database management program more effective and easier to use.

You can create a form with the help of AutoForm or the Form Wizard, or you can create a form from scratch in Design view.

Exhibit 6-1: A sample Access form

Examining a form in Design view

To create a form or change its design, you can use Design view, shown in Exhibit 6-2. In Design view, a form contains three main areas:

- **Form Header** — Here, you can enter a heading that describes the form's purpose. This header appears at the top of the form for every record.
- **Detail** — The Detail area contains various controls, such as label and text box controls.
- **Form Footer** — Here, you can enter any information that you want to display at the bottom of a form when the form is previewed or printed.

The Form Header and Form Footer sections might not be visible when you open a form in Design view. You can show or hide them by choosing View, Form Header/Footer.

When you open a form in Design view, a toolbox appears with controls that you can use to change the form's appearance. If you're not using the toolbox, you can close it by clicking the Close button.

The following table describes some of the commonly used controls in the toolbox:

Control	Name	Description
Aa	Label	Used to give a description for the controls used in a form.
ab|	Text box	Used to enter data, such as numbers or text.
⊙	Option button	Used to select a single option from a given set of options.
☑	Check box	Used to select multiple options from a given list of options.
	Combo box	Used to select an option from a drop-down list.
	List box	Used to select multiple options from a list.

Form Design view also contains a field list, which shows all the fields in the table on which the form is based. To display the fields, you can choose View, Field List or click the Field List button on the Form Design toolbar.

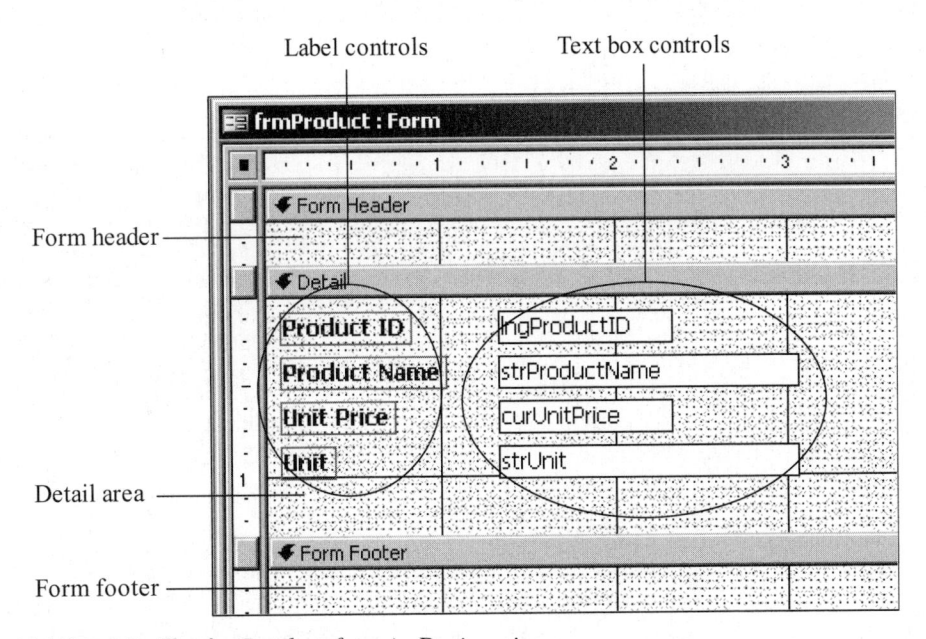

Exhibit 6-2: The frmProduct form in Design view

Do it!

A-1: Examining a form

Here's how	Here's why
1 Open CreateForm	From the current unit folder.
2 On the Objects bar, click **Forms**	(If necessary.) You'll examine a form.
3 Select **frmProduct**	
4 Click **Design**	(The Design button is on the Database toolbar.) To open frmProduct in Design view.
5 Choose **View**, **Form Header/Footer**	To show the Form Header and Form Footer sections.
Choose **View**, **Form Header/Footer**	To hide the header and footer again.
6 Observe the toolbox	It contains various controls that can be used in forms.
7 Observe the form	The form contains the Detail area. The label controls—such as Product ID, Product Name, Unit Price, and Unit—are on the left side of the window.
8 Observe the text box controls	The field names appear in the text boxes. The form gets the values for these fields from the source table. You can see the values when you switch to Form view.
9 Close the window	Choose File, Close. If a message box appears, click No to close without saving changes.

The AutoForm feature

Explanation

If you're using the AutoForm feature to create a form, all fields appear automatically in the form. There are two ways to create a form by using this feature:

- On the Database toolbar, click the New Object button.
- On the Objects bar, click Forms, click New, and select AutoForm: Columnar or AutoForm: Tabular.

If you use the New Object button to create a form, the layout of the form is always columnar. After creating the form, AutoForm displays the form in Form view. A columnar form displays values in one or more columns, as shown in Exhibit 6-3. A tabular form displays values in a row and column format. After creating a form with AutoForm, you can arrange the controls to better suit your needs.

A *control* is an object in a form that displays data, allows you to edit data, or performs some action. For example, the form shown in Exhibit 6-3 contains label controls and text box controls. Label controls display field names, and text box controls display the data contained in the fields.

Text box controls are an example of *bound controls;* they are linked to the fields of the underlying source table. Any change made in a bound control is reflected in the underlying data source. For example, if you're working in a form, and you change data entered in a text box, the underlying field is also changed.

Label controls are an example of *unbound controls;* they are stand-alone controls that do not have a data source. Use unbound controls to display information (such as labels), lines, rectangles, and pictures.

To create a form by using the AutoForm feature:

1. Open the database.
2. Select the table on which to base the form.
3. Click the New Object: AutoForm button on the Database toolbar to create a form.
4. Save the form.

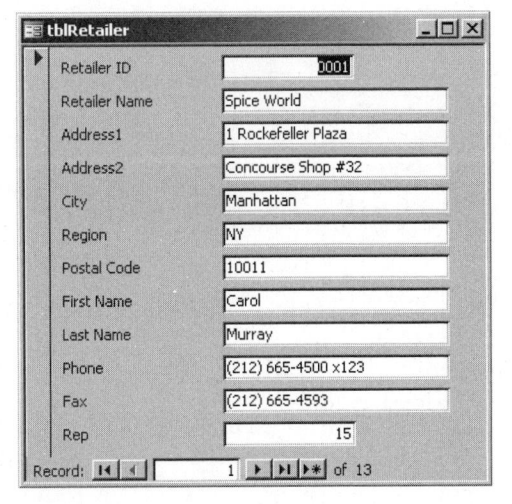

Exhibit 6-3: The Form view window

Do it!

A-2: Creating a form by using AutoForm

Here's how	Here's why
1 On the Objects bar, click **Tables**	You'll select the underlying source table for a form.
2 Select **tblRetailer**	(If necessary.) To specify the name of the table on which the form will be based.
3 Click [icon]	(The New Object button is on the Database toolbar.) To create the form and view it in Form view. The first record appears in a columnar form, as shown in Exhibit 6-3.
4 Choose **File**, **Save As...**	To open the Save As dialog box.
5 Edit the Save Form 'Form1' To box to read **frmAutoForm** In the As list, verify that Form appears	To name the form.
6 Click **OK**	To save the form.

Navigating forms

Explanation

In Form view, the navigation buttons help you to move through the records. These buttons and a record number box, shown in Exhibit 6-4, are located on the navigation bar below the form.

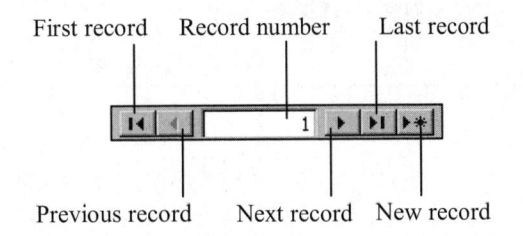

Exhibit 6-4: The navigation buttons and the record number box

Do it!

A-3: Using the navigation bar

Here's how	Here's why
1 Verify that frmAutoForm is open in Form view	
2 Click ▶	(The next record button is on the navigation bar.) To move to the next record.
3 Click ▶❘	(The last record button.) To move to the last record.
4 Click ❘◀	(The first record button.) To move to the first record.

Entering data in a form

Explanation

You can enter and edit data in a form. You can edit existing records, or add a blank record by clicking the new record button on the navigation bar.

Do it!

A-4: Using a form for data entry

Here's how	Here's why
1 Click ▶*	(The new record button is on the navigation bar.) To create a new record. A blank record appears.
2 Enter data as shown	Retailer Name: Magic Spices Address1: 111 SE Carnegie St Address2: City: Astoria Region: OR Postal Code: 97102
3 Update and close the form	
4 On the Objects bar, click **Forms**	(If necessary.) To see the name of the form in the Database window. The frmAutoForm form appears in the Database window, indicating that the form you created has been saved as a form object in the database.

Topic B: Using the Form Wizard

This topic covers the following Microsoft Office Specialist exam objective.

#	Objective
AC03S-1-7	Creating forms using the Form Wizard

The Form Wizard

Explanation

You can also create a form by using the Form Wizard. In the Form Wizard, you can select the fields you want to display, the order in which the fields will appear, a layout, and a style. The Form Wizard guides you through the steps necessary to create a form. The difference between the Form Wizard and the AutoForm feature is that the Form Wizard helps you specify which fields you want in the form, whereas AutoForm automatically places all of a table's fields in the form.

To create a form by using the Form Wizard:

1. On the Objects bar of the Database window, click Forms. Click the New button on the Database window toolbar to open the New Form dialog box.
2. In the dialog box, first select Form Wizard, and then select the table on which you want to base the form, as shown in Exhibit 6-5. Click OK to open the Form Wizard dialog box.
3. Select the fields that you want to display in the form. Click Next to move to the next step of the Form Wizard.
4. Select a form layout. Click Next.
5. Select a style for the form. Click Next.
6. Enter a title for the form. Then click Finish to close the dialog box and save the form.

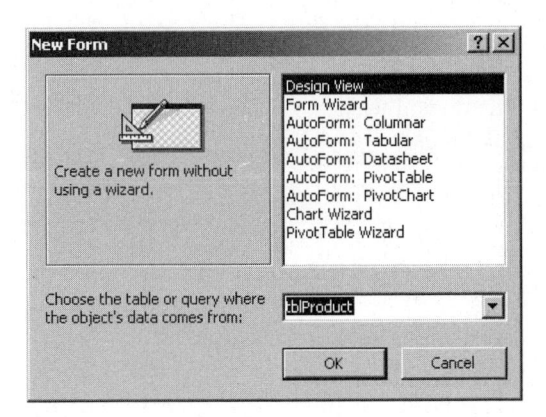

Exhibit 6-5: The New Form dialog box

B-1: Creating a form by using the Form Wizard

Do it!

Here's how	Here's why
1 Click **New**	(The New button is on the Database window toolbar.) To open the New Form dialog box. By default, Design view is selected.
2 Select **Form Wizard**	To create a form by using the Form Wizard.
3 From the Choose table or query where the object's data comes from list, select **tblProduct**	To specify the name of the table on which your form will be based.
4 Click **OK**	(To display the Form Wizard.) Under Tables/Queries, Table: tblProduct is selected, and under Available Fields, all fields of the tblProduct table are listed.
5 Under Available Fields, verify that lngProductID is selected	You'll add this field to the Selected Fields list.
Click `>`	(To add lngProductID to the Selected Fields list.) lngProductID appears in the Selected Fields list.
6 Click `>>`	To add all the fields to the Selected Fields list.
7 Click **Next**	The wizard now displays form layout options.
8 Verify that Columnar is selected	You'll create a columnar form.
9 Click **Next**	The wizard now displays various form styles. By default, Standard is selected.
Click **Next**	
10 Edit the What title do you want for your form box to read **frmFormWizard**	This will be the form's title.
Click **Finish**	
	The form appears in Form view, displaying the first record. The record is shown in a columnar layout.

11	Click ▶	To view the next record in the form.
	Click ▶▮	To view the last record in the form.
	Close the form	The frmFormWizard appears in the Database window.

Topic C: Using Design view

This topic covers the following Microsoft Office Specialist exam objectives.

#	Objective
AC03S-1-9	Modifying form properties
AC03S-1-9	Modifying specific form controls (.e.g., text boxes, labels, bound controls) (This objective is also covered in *Access 2003: Intermediate*, in the units titled "Working with related tables" and "Advanced form design.")
AC03S-3-2	Showing and hiding headers and footers

Creating forms in Design view

Explanation

After creating a form by using Form Wizard or AutoForm, you can open it in Design view. Here, you can add, remove, resize, and rearrange the controls, as well as change the form's colors. You can also create a new form from scratch in Design view.

To create a form in Design view:

1 On the Objects bar of the Database window, click Forms. Click New to open the New Form dialog box.
2 In the dialog box, first select Design View if necessary, and then select the table on which you want to base the form. Click OK to open the Form1: Form window.
3 From the field list, drag the fields you want to use, and place them on the form.
4 From the toolbox, drag the controls you want to use, and place them on the form.
5 Choose File, Save As to save the form.

Using forms **6-13**

Showing the header and footer section

To show the Form Header and Form Footer sections, choose View, Form Header/Footer.

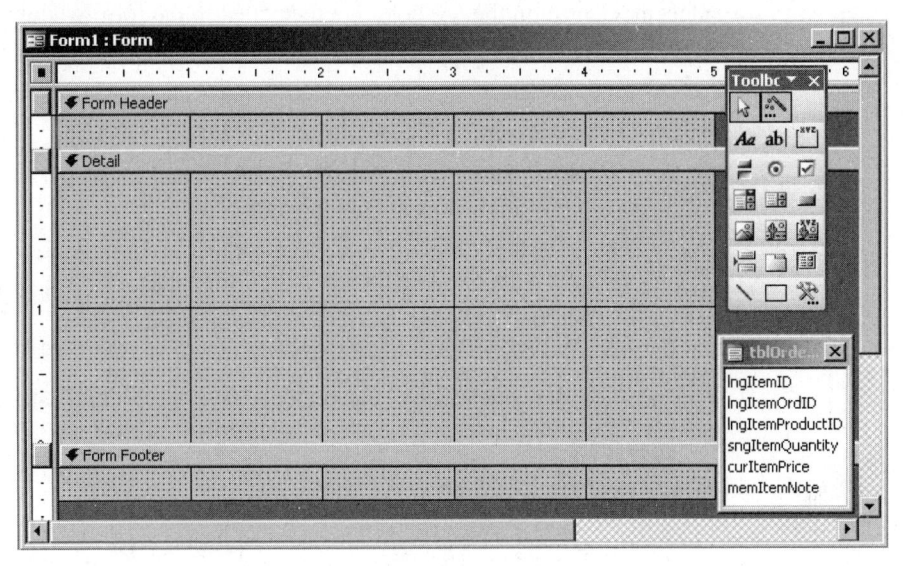

Exhibit 6-6: The form after Step 5 of the activity

Do it!

C-1: Creating a form in Design view

Here's how	Here's why
1 On the Objects bar, verify that Forms is selected	
2 Click **New**	To open the New Form dialog box.
Verify that Design View is selected	
3 From the Choose the table or query where the object's data comes from list, select **tblOrderItem**	To specify the table on which you'll base the form.
4 Click **OK**	To display the Design view window. The field list also appears.
5 Choose **View, Form Header/Footer**	To show the Form Header and Form Footer sections. These sections appear in the form, as shown in Exhibit 6-6.

6–14   Access 2003: Basic

Form titles

Explanation

The title of the form will appear at the top of the form. You can add a title to the Form Header section by using a label control. To place a label or text box control in a form, select the control in the toolbox, and then click in the form where you want to place the control. You can then format the text of the label control.

To add a title to a form:

1. Click the Form Header section.
2. Click the Toolbox button on the Form Design toolbar to display the toolbox.
3. Select the label control from the toolbox.
4. Place the label control in the Form Header section by clicking where you want to place the control. Drag the label until it reaches the size you want; then release the mouse button.
5. Enter the title in the label control.

You can modify the header by selecting the label control and using the desired buttons (such as Font, Font Size, and Bold) on the Formatting toolbar.

Do it!

C-2:   Adding a title to a form

Here's how	Here's why
1 Place the mouse pointer over the top edge of the Detail section, and drag the Detail bar as shown	(To increase the size of the Form Header section.) The pointer changes to a double-headed arrow.
2 Click [toolbox icon]	(If necessary) To display the toolbox. The Toolbox button is on the Form Design toolbar.
3 Click [Aa]	(The Label button is in the toolbox.) To add a label control to the form.
Point in the Form Header area as shown	The pointer changes to a crosshair with the letter A.

4	Drag as shown	
		To create the label control.
5	In the label control, enter **Order Details**	This will be the form's title.
6	Click anywhere on the form	(To deselect the title.) Notice that the buttons on the Formatting toolbar are no longer available. "Order Details" appears as the heading for the form.
7	Select the Order Details label control	
		The buttons on the Formatting toolbar are now available.
8	From the Font Size list, select **12**	(The Font Size list is on the Formatting toolbar.) To increase the font size.
	From the Font list, select **Arial**	(The Font list is on the Formatting toolbar.) To change the font.
	Click **B**	(The Bold button is on the Formatting toolbar.) To make the title bold.
9	Close the toolbox	
10	Save the form as **frmDesign**	Choose File, Save As.

6–16 Access 2003: Basic

Working with controls

Explanation   You can move and resize controls in Design view. To place a new label control or a text box control in the form, you can select a field from the field list and drag it to the Detail section. The shape of the pointer changes to a field box. Both controls appear in the location to which you dragged the field.

When you select either control (label or text box), the shape of the pointer changes to a hand, and handles appear around the control. *Handles* are small, black rectangles around the control. You change the size of a control by dragging the handles, and you move a control by dragging the whole control when the pointer changes to a hand.

Do it!   **C-3: Adding controls**

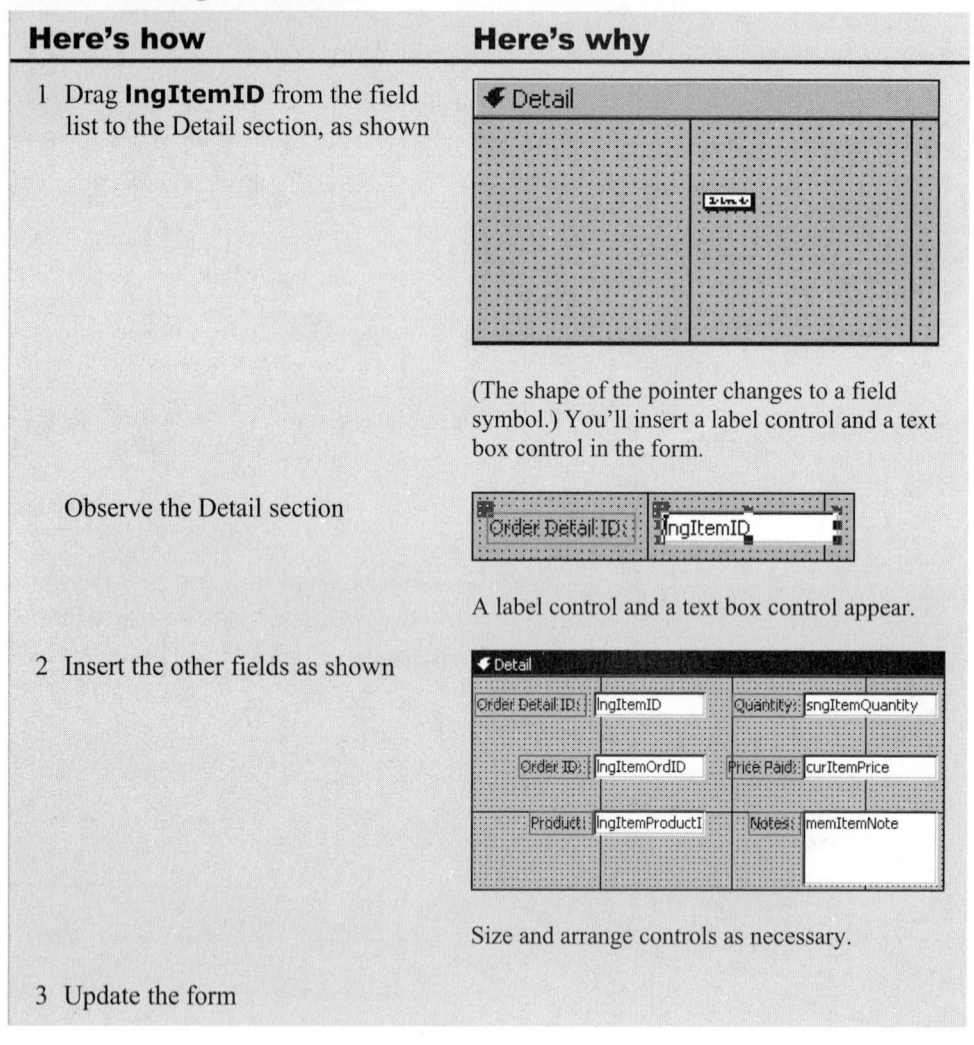

Here's how	Here's why
1 Drag **lngItemID** from the field list to the Detail section, as shown	
	(The shape of the pointer changes to a field symbol.) You'll insert a label control and a text box control in the form.
Observe the Detail section	
	A label control and a text box control appear.
2 Insert the other fields as shown	
	Size and arrange controls as necessary.
3 Update the form	

Form control properties

Explanation

Each control in a form has a set of properties, which determine its appearance and behavior. All controls have a *property sheet*, which is used to change or customize the properties, such as Caption and Font Name. The property sheet contains five tabs: Format, Data, Event, Other, and All.

Section properties

Each section of the form also has its own properties and property sheet. For example, you can change the background color of the Form Header by changing the Back Color property on the Form Header section property sheet, which is shown in Exhibit 6-7.

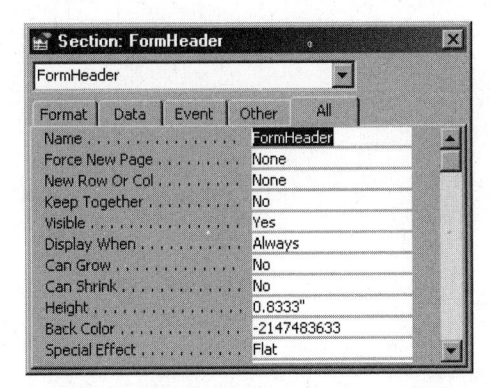

Exhibit 6-7: The property sheet for the Form Header section

Modifying section properties

To modify section properties:

1. Select the section of the form for which you want to modify the properties.
2. Click the Properties button on the Form Design toolbar to display the property sheet.
3. In the property sheet, change the section properties, as you want.
4. Update the form.

Do it! **C-4: Modifying properties**

Here's how	Here's why
1 Click anywhere in the Form Header section	You'll modify the properties of the Form Header section.
2 Click	(The Properties button is on the Form Design toolbar.) To display the property sheet.
3 Verify that the All tab is activated	The list in the property sheet displays FormHeader. This list displays the name of the selected control or section whose properties are being modified. The property sheet displays the properties of the Form Header section.
4 Place the insertion point in the Back Color box	A button appears to the right of the Back Color box.
5 Click	To display the Color palette and view the various colors.
Select any shade of yellow	To change the background color of the Form Header section to yellow.
Click **OK**	
6 Place the insertion point in the Special Effect box	A drop-down arrow appears.
Click the arrow	To display a list.
From the list, select **Raised**	You'll change the appearance of the Form Header section.
7 Close the property sheet	Click the Close button in the property sheet.

8	Click anywhere in the Detail section	You'll modify the properties of the Detail section.
9	Press [F4]	To open the property sheet.
10	Change the background color of the Detail section to yellow	
11	Select the label **Quantity**	Notice the property sheet changes. You don't need to close the sheet between selections.
	Click the **Format** tab	
	Edit the Caption box to read **Quantity sold:**	This will be the new caption of the label.
	Resize the Quantity label	(If necessary.) So you can see all the text.
12	Close the property sheet	
13	Switch to Form view	(Click the View button on the Form Design toolbar.) The modified form appears.
14	Update and close the form	

6–20 Access 2003: Basic

Property inheritance propagation

Explanation

If you change the format of fields in a table after you have created objects based on that table, you need those existing objects to reflect the changes in the table. To do so, you use the *property inheritance propagation* feature. For example, if you change the format of the dtmOrderDate field in the tblOrder table, you can have the change reflected in the frmOrder form by using property inheritance propagation.

Do it!

C-5: Inheriting properties

Here's how	Here's why
1 In the Objects bar, click **Tables**	If necessary.
2 Open tblOrder in Design view	
3 Display the general properties for the field dtmOrderDate	You'll change the format of this field.
4 From the Format list, select **Medium Date**	(To change the format of the date.) A smart tag appears.
5 Click as shown	
Observe the Property Update Options menu	The Property Update Options menu appears. The menu contains options to update the format of the dtmOrderDate field in all the objects where it's used.
6 Choose the option as shown	The Update Properties dialog box appears.
7 Observe the dialog box	It lists the names of all the objects that contain the dtmOrderDate field.
Click **Yes**	To update the format of the dtmOrderDate field in the frmOrder form.
8 Update and close the window	

9	On the Objects bar, click **Forms**	
10	Open frmOrder	The format of the date in the Order Date field has changed to Medium Date.
	Close the window	

Topic D: Finding, sorting, and filtering records

This topic covers the following Microsoft Office Specialist exam objectives.

#	Objective
AC03S-3-5	Sorting records in tables, queries, forms and reports (This objective is also covered in the units titled "Fields and records," "Simple queries," and "Working with reports.")
AC03S-3-6	Filtering datasheets by form (This objective is also covered in the unit titled "Fields and records.")

Using a form to locate information

Explanation

You can use the Find, Sort, and Filter features in a form. For example, you can sort the records in a form so as to view the retailers alphabetically by retailer name. You can also restrict the modification of selected records by filtering out records that you don't want modified.

Using Find

You can search for a record by clicking the Find button or by choosing Edit, Find. Before searching for a record, ensure that the form is on the first record, because the search operation always starts from the current record.

To find a record:

1. In the form, place the insertion point in the field in which you want to find a value.
2. Click Find to open the Find and Replace dialog box. Verify that the Find tab is activated.
3. In the Find What box, enter the value you want to find.
4. Click Find Next to display the records containing that value.
5. Click OK to close the message box. Click Cancel to close the Find and Replace dialog box.

Do it! **D-1: Using a form to find records**

Here's how	Here's why
1 Open frmProduct in Form view	You'll search for specific records in this form.
2 Place the insertion point in the Unit Price text box	You'll find records based on Unit Price.
3 Click 🔍	(The Find button is on the Form View toolbar.) To open the Find and Replace dialog box. The Find tab is activated, and the insertion point is in the Find What box.
4 In the Find What box, enter **$1.75**, as shown	You'll search records for this value. Notice that Unit Price is selected in the Look In list, indicating the field to be searched.
In the Match list, verify that Whole Field is selected	To specify that the entire field has to be matched.
In the Search list, verify that All is selected	To specify that all the records are to be searched.
5 Click **Find Next**	To display the result in Form view. A record with a Unit Price of $1.75 appears in the form.
6 Click **Find Next**	A message box appears, stating that the searched item was not found.
7 Click **OK**	To close the message box.
8 Click **Cancel**	To close the Find and Replace dialog box.
Close the form	

Sorting records by using a form

Explanation

You can use a form to sort records in a table in either ascending or descending order.

If you want to arrange the records in ascending order, select the field on which you want to sort, and click the Sort Ascending button on the Form View toolbar. Otherwise, click the Sort Descending button.

Do it!

D-2: Using a form to sort records

Here's how	Here's why
1 Open frmRetailer in Form view	The records are sorted based on the Retailer ID, which is the primary key.
Place the insertion point in the Retailer Name box	You'll sort the records based on Retailer Name.
2 Click [A/Z↓]	(The Sort Ascending button is on the Form View toolbar.) To sort the records in ascending order. You'll see the first record after sorting. The records are now sorted based on the Retailer Name field.
3 Navigate through records	The records are now sorted alphabetically by retailer name.
Return to the first record	
4 Update the form	

Using forms **6–25**

Filtering records by using a form

Explanation

You can selectively view the records in a form by using the Filter By Form feature. For example, you can set the filter to view the products sold in a specific location. The Filter By Form feature contains two tabs: Look for, and Or. The Look for tab is used to filter records. The Or tab is used to enter alternate values, which are displayed by using the Look for tab.

To apply a filter:
1. On the Form View toolbar, click Filter By Form.
2. Select the field on which you want to set the filter.
3. Select the value for setting the filter from the available list.
4. Click Apply Filter.

Do it!

D-3: Using a form to filter records

Here's how	Here's why
1 Click [icon]	(The Filter By Form button is on the Form View toolbar.) To display a blank frmRetailer form. A drop-down arrow appears next to the Retailer ID box. The Look for tab is activated at the bottom of the form.
2 Place the insertion point in the Retailer Name box	A drop-down arrow now appears next to the Retailer Name box.
3 Enter **S***	You'll view the records for only retailer names starting with S.
Press (TAB)	In the Retailer Name box, Like "S*" appears. You're using the * wildcard operator to filter data.
4 Click [icon]	(The Apply Filter button is on the Form View toolbar.) To apply the filter. The first record in the filtered set of records appears. The bottom of the form shows the total number of filtered records.
Navigate through the records	Notice all the retailer names start with S.
5 Update and close the form	
6 Close the database	

Unit summary: Using forms

Topic A In this topic, you examined a form in **Design view**. You also created a form by using the **AutoForm** feature. In addition, you learned how to navigate in a form by using the navigation bar. You entered **a record** in a form.

Topic B In this topic, you created a form by using the **Form Wizard**. You learned that the difference between the Form Wizard and AutoForm is that when you use the Form Wizard, you can specify the fields you want on the form, whereas the AutoForm feature automatically places all the table's fields on the form.

Topic C In this topic, you learned how to create a form in **Design view**. You created a customized form by moving, adding, or rearranging **controls** in the form in Design view. You also changed the appearance of a form by modifying its **properties**.

Topic D In this topic, you learned how to use forms to **find**, **sort**, and **filter** records. You arranged records and worked with specific records by sorting and filtering records.

Independent practice activity

1. Open Employee.
2. Create a columnar form based on the tblEmployee table by using the AutoForm feature.
3. Enter a new record in the form, as shown in Exhibit 6-8.
4. Save the form as **frmEmployeeDetails** and close it.
5. Using the Form Wizard, create a form based on the tblEmployee table.
6. Select all the fields in the table, and create a tabular form based on the Industrial style.
7. Save the form as **frmEmployee**. Compare the form to Exhibit 6-9.
8. Close frmEmployee.
9. Create a form in Design view using tblOrderItem.
10. Enter **Sales Analysis** as the title. The size and font of the title should be 14 and Arial. (*Hint:* Choose View, Form Header/Footer to display the form header and footer.)
11. Set the background color of the title to green, and set the border color to yellow. (*Hint:* You might need to scroll to see the Border property.)
12. Drag fields from the fields list to create the form as shown in Exhibit 6-10.
13. Sort the records in ascending order by Product. (*Hint:* You must be in Form view.)
14. Filter the records based on the Quantity field for values greater than 200. (*Hint:* Enter >200 in the Quantity field.)
15. Save the form as **frmSalesAnalysis**.
16. Close the form and the database.

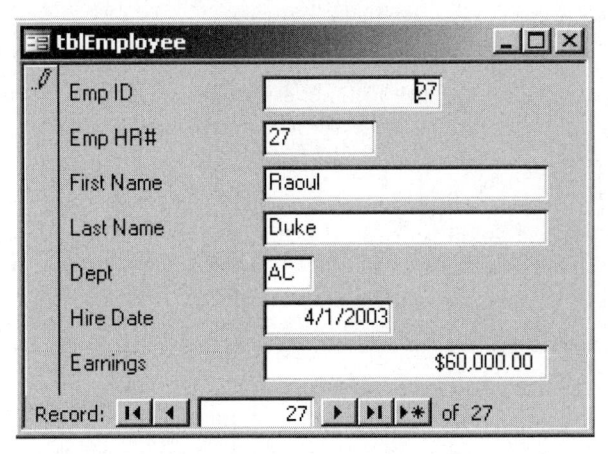

Exhibit 6-8: The frmEmployeeDetails form after Step 3 of the Independent Practice Activity

Exhibit 6-9: A sample of frmEmployee after Step 7 of the Independent Practice Activity

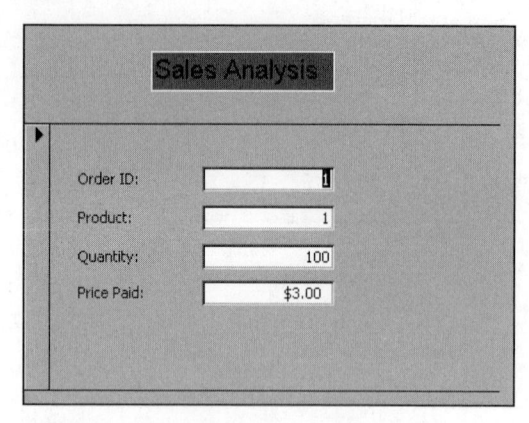

Exhibit 6-10: A sample of the Sales Analysis form after Step 12 of the Independent Practice Activity

Review questions

1 Which view is used to create or modify a form?

2 What are the three main areas of a form?

3 Identify the following controls that can be used when designing forms.

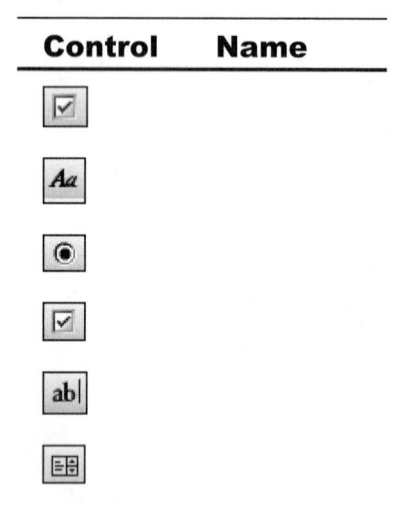

Control	Name
☑	
Aa	
⦿	
☑	
ab|	
🗐	

4 Name two ways to create a form by using AutoForm feature.

5 What is the difference between bound and unbound controls?

6 What is the difference between creating a form with the AutoForm feature and creating a form with the Form Wizard?

7 How do you add a title to a form?

8 Which of the following is used to manage the appearance and behavior of a form control?.

   A Toolbox

   B Control handles

   C Text box

   D Property sheet

9 How do you sort records by form?

10 How do you use a form to filter records?

Unit 7
Working with reports

Unit time: 50 minutes

Complete this unit, and you'll know how to:

A Create reports by using AutoReport, Report Wizard, Design view, and queries.

B Group and sort records in a report, summarize information in a report, change the report layout and style, and print a report.

Topic A: Creating reports

This topic covers the following Microsoft Office Specialist exam objectives.

#	Objective
AC03S-1-10	Creating reports
AC03S-4-2	Previewing for print (This objective is also covered in Topic B.)

Explanation

Reports

A *report* is an Access database object that presents data in an organized format suitable for viewing on screen or printing. Access creates a report by using the underlying source table or query, and Access can run calculations on fields and group data by specified criteria. In Exhibit 7-1, the Product Details report shows the records from the tblProduct table. A report is not used to enter or edit data.

The commonly used methods to create reports are using AutoReport, using the Report Wizard, and using Design view. AutoReport generates a report that contains all the fields of the source table. The Report Wizard prompts you to select the fields you want to include in the report. Design view gives you the flexibility to design customized reports from the ground up.

Viewing a report

To view an existing report, you click Reports on the Objects bar, select a report object, and click Preview. To preview a report, you must have a printer driver installed on your computer. A report contains a report heading and various column headings for the fields.

You can view one page of a report at a time. In the report preview, the pointer changes to a magnifying glass so that you can switch between Pages and Zoom views. In Pages view, one page of a report fits on screen, while Zoom view shows an enlarged report.

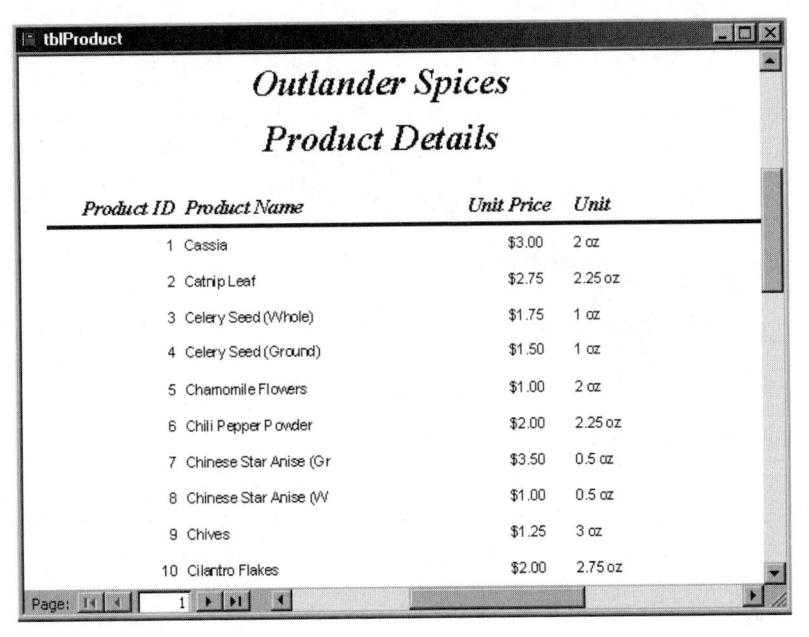

Exhibit 7-1: The Product Details report

Do it! **A-1: Examining a report**

Here's how	Here's why
1 Open CreateReport	(From the current unit folder.) If a message box appears, click Enable Macros.
2 Click **Reports**	(On the Objects bar.) You'll examine a report.
3 Select **rptProduct**	If necessary.
Click **Preview**	(The Preview button is on the Database window toolbar.) To open the report preview.
Maximize the window	
4 Point to the report area	The pointer changes to a magnifying glass. You can use it to switch between Pages and Zoom views.
Click in the report area	To zoom in on the report.
Observe the Preview window	(As shown in Exhibit 7-1.) It contains both vertical and horizontal scrollbars that you can use to scroll through the report.
5 Observe the headings	The report heading is Outlander Spices Product Details, and the field headings include Product ID, Product Name, Unit Price, and Unit.
Observe the end of the report	(Scroll down.) The current date appears on the left side.
Point anywhere on the report, and click	To zoom out on the report.
6 Restore and close the report window	Click the Restore Window button and then the Close button.

Using AutoReport

Explanation

There are two ways to start using AutoReport:
- On the Database toolbar, click the New Object button.
- On the Objects bar, click Reports, click New, and select AutoReport: Columnar or AutoReport: Tabular.

If you use the New Object button to create a report, the layout is always columnar. After creating the report, AutoReport displays the report in Print Preview. A columnar report displays values in one or more columns. A tabular report displays values in a row and column format.

To create a report by using AutoReport:

1. Open the database.
2. On the Objects bar, click Reports.
3. Click New to open the New Report dialog box.
4. In the dialog box, first select AutoReport: Columnar or AutoReport: Tabular. Then select the table on which you want to base the report, as shown in Exhibit 7-2.
5. Click OK.

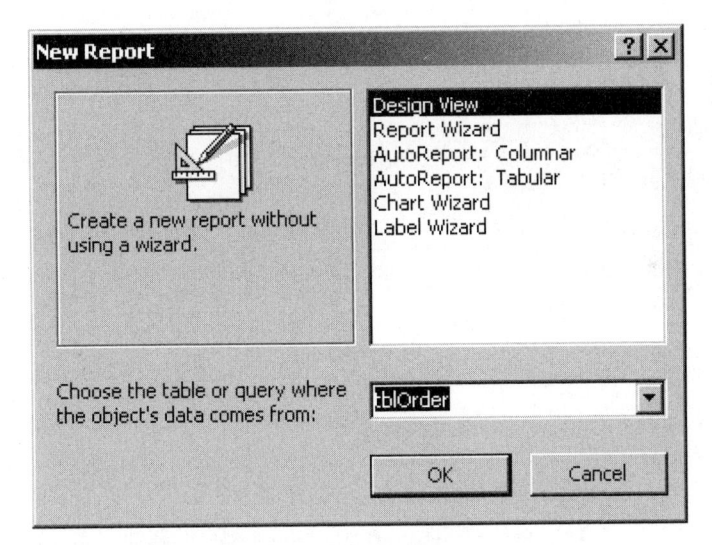

Exhibit 7-2: The New Report dialog box

Do it!

A-2: Creating reports by using AutoReport

Here's how	Here's why
1 Click **Reports**	(On the Objects bar.) You'll create a new AutoReport.
2 Click **New**	To open the New Report window
Select **AutoReport: Columnar** from the list	
From the drop-down list, select **tblOrder**	To specify the table on which the report will be based.
Click **OK**	To create the report and open a preview.
3 Choose **File**, **Save As…**	To open the Save As dialog box.
Edit the Save Report 'Report1' To box to read **rptAutoReport**	To name the report.
Verify that Report appears in the As list	
4 Click **OK**	To save the report.
5 Close the window	Choose File, Close.
6 On the Objects bar, click **Reports**	The rptAutoReport appears in the Database window.

The Report Wizard

Explanation

When you create a report by using the Report Wizard, you can specify the fields you want to include in the report, and you can arrange the data by specifying a condition for sorting the records. You can also include summary calculations in your report. The Report Wizard guides you through every step of designing a report, from selecting fields to choosing a style, such as Corporate, Formal, or Casual, for the printed page. The *style* defines how the title and other information will appear in a report.

To create a report by using the Report Wizard:

1 On the Objects bar, click Reports. Click New on the Database window toolbar to open the New Report dialog box.
2 Select Report Wizard. Then, from the data source list, select a table on which the report will be based. Click OK to open the Report Wizard.
3 From the Available Fields list, select the fields you want to include in the report. Click Next.
4 Select the options you need from the remaining steps of the Report Wizard.
5 Click Finish to exit the Wizard and create the report.

rptOrderDetails

IngItemOrdID	Product · Detail ID		Quantity	Price Paid	Notes
1					
	1	1	100	$3.00	
	11	13	50	$4.25	
	12	11	150	$5.50	
2					
	3	2	400	$1.75	
	7	12	20	$3.50	
3					
	5	3	200	$1.00	
4					
	2	4	200	$2.75	
	3	14	200	$1.75	
	28	15	200	$1.89	
	34	16	2	$17.00	

Exhibit 7-3: The preview of the rptOrderDetails report

Do it!

A-3: Creating reports by using the Report Wizard

Here's how	Here's why
1 Click **New**	(The New button is on the Database window toolbar.) To open the New Report dialog box.
Observe the dialog box	Design View is selected, by default.
2 Select **Report Wizard**	You'll create a report by using the Report Wizard.
3 From the drop-down list, select **tblOrderItem**	You'll create a report based on this table.
4 Click **OK**	To open the Report Wizard. In the Tables/Queries list, Table: tblOrderItem is selected.
5 In the Available Fields list, verify that lngItemID is selected	
6 Click `>`	(The Add button is on the Report Wizard dialog box.) To add lngItemID to the Selected Fields list.
7 Click `>>`	(To add all the fields.) Now all the fields appear in the Selected Fields list.
8 Click **Next**	To move to the next step of the Report Wizard. The Grouping Options button is not active because you have not yet selected any field for grouping.
9 Select **lngItemOrdID**	You'll view records grouped on this field.
10 Click `>`	To add lngItemOrdID to the grouping levels. lngItemOrdID appears in a separate box in the top pane. Notice that the Grouping Options button is now active.
11 Click **Next**	
Observe the Wizard	(The insertion point is in the first list.) You use this screen to specify the field on which you want to sort the records in the report.

Working with reports   **7–9**

12	From the first list, select **lngItemProductID**		To sort records by lngItemProductID in ascending order.
13	Click **Next**		To move to the next step of the Report Wizard. The various report layouts appear.
14	Under Layout, verify that Stepped is selected		To specify a layout for the report.
15	Under Orientation, verify that Portrait is selected		To specify the orientation of the report.
16	Verify that Adjust the field width so all fields fit on a page is checked		
17	Click **Next**		To move to the next step of the Report Wizard. The different report styles appear.
18	Select **Corporate**		(If necessary.) To specify a style for the report.
	Click **Next**		
19	Edit the What title do you want for your report? box to read **rptOrderDetails**		To specify the report's title.
	Verify that Preview the report is selected		To preview the report on screen before printing it.
	Click **Finish**		You'll see a preview of the report, as shown in Exhibit 7-3. The title of the report is rptOrderDetails. The report shows records from the tblOrderItem table that are grouped by lngItemOrdID and sorted by lngItemProductID.
20	Choose **File**, **Close**		To close the report.

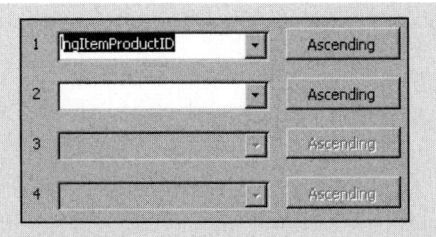

Creating reports in Design view

Explanation

Design view provides you with various tools to design reports. Tools include the Formatting toolbar, the toolbox, the field list, and the property sheet.

Report Design view

Report Design view is divided into seven sections: Report Header, Page Header, Group Header, Detail, Group Footer, Page Footer, and Report Footer. These sections are used to control the location of the report elements. For example, the controls in the Report Header section appear at the beginning of a report. The following table describes each section:

Section	Description
Report Header	Appears at the top of the first page of the report. Use this section to show a company logo, the report name, or the date.
Page Header	Appears at the top of every page of the report. It appears below the report header on the first page. Use this section to show the field headings.
Group Header	Appears before every group of records. A group in a report contains records arranged together based on a specific field value. Use this section to display information, such as a group name, that applies to the entire group. For example, you can group records based on products sold to a customer, and the group heading can contain the name of that customer.
Detail	Appears once for every record. This section contains the main body of the report and is repeated for each record in the report's source table or query.
Group Footer	Appears at the end of a group of records. Use this section to show information, such as group totals, that is specific to every group.
Page Footer	Appears at the end of every page of the report. Use this section to show information such as page numbers and dates.
Report Footer	Appears at the end of the report before the page footer of the last page. Use this section to show information such as grand totals.

Working with reports **7-11**

Do it! **A-4: Creating a report by using Design view**

Here's how	Here's why
1 On the Objects bar, verify that Reports is selected	You'll create a report in Design view.
2 Click **New**	(The New button is on the Database window toolbar.) To open the New Report dialog box.
Verify that Design View is selected	
From the drop-down list, select **tblRetailer**	To select the table on which the report will be based.
3 Click **OK**	To open the Design view window. The three sections Page Header, Detail, and Page Footer appear.
4 Drag the Detail bar as shown	
	(To increase the size of the Page Header section.) The pointer changes to a double-headed arrow.
5 Click	(If necessary.) To display the toolbox.
6 Click **Aa**	(The Label button is on the toolbox.) To add a label control to the form.
7 Point in the Page Header area as shown	
Drag as shown	

8	In the label control, enter **Retailer Details**	This will be the report's title.
	Press `← ENTER`	This will exit editing mode and select the control.
	Use the formatting toolbar to make the title 14pt and Bold	
9	Drag **lngRetailerID** from the field list to the Detail section, as shown	
	Observe the Detail section	
		A label control and a text box control appear.
10	Insert other fields as shown	
11	Save the report as **rptRetailerDetails**	
12	Close the window	Notice that rptRetailerDetails appears in the Database window.
13	Select rptRetailerDetails	
	Click Preview	To view the report.
14	Close the report	

Creating reports based on queries

Explanation

To create a report based on a query, either select an existing query or create a new one in Design view. You can then use AutoReport to create the report based on this query.

To create a report based on a query:

1 On the Objects bar, click Queries.
2 Select the query on which you'll base the report.
3 Open the query in Design view.
4 Click the down arrow next to the New Object: AutoForm button. From the list, select Report to open the New Report dialog box.
5 In the dialog box, select one of the AutoReport options: Tabular or Columnar. Click OK to preview the report.

You can also use the New Report dialog box to create a report based on a query. In the New Report dialog box, select either AutoReport: Columnar or AutoReport: Tabular. Then, from the data source list, select the query on which you'll base the report. Click OK.

A-5: Creating a report by using a query

Do it!

Here's how	Here's why
1 Open qryOrderItem in Design view	(On the Objects bar, click Queries, and select qryOrderItem. Then, click the Design button.) You'll create a report based on this query.
Observe the design grid	

Field:	lngItemOrdID	lngItemProductID	sngItemQuantity	curItemPrice
Table:	tblOrderItem	tblOrderItem	tblOrderItem	tblOrderItem
Sort:				
Show:	☑	☑	☑	☑
Criteria:			<50	

	The query is based on the tblOrderItem table. There are four fields in the design grid. The Criteria cell of sngItemQuantity contains <50. This indicates that this query will display records containing values < 50 in the sngItemQuantity field.
2 Click the arrow next to the New Object button, as shown	
	(The New Object button is on the Query Design toolbar.) To display a menu of database objects.
3 From the menu, choose **Report**	(You'll create a report based on the query qryOrderItem.) To open the New Report dialog box. The query qryOrderItem is already in the drop-down list.
4 Select **AutoReport: Tabular**	You'll create a tabular report.
5 Click **OK**	To create and display the report.
Observe the report	

qryOrderItem

Order ID	Product	Quantity	Price Paid
2	7	20	$3.50
4	34	2	$17.00
5	23	25	$1.23
6	33	4	$14.89
11	29	20	$12.49
11	30	20	$1.89
14	29	10	$12.49

	The records that meet the criterion appear in the report. The report heading is automatically placed at the top and is the same as the source query name. You can modify this later in Design view.
6 Click **Close**	(The Close button is on the Print Preview toolbar.) The report appears in Design view.
7 Save the report as **rptSalesReport**	

Topic B: Modifying and printing reports

This topic covers the following Microsoft Office Specialist exam objectives.

#	Objective
AC03S-3-3	Aligning, resizing, and spacing controls (This objective is also covered in *Access 2003: Intermediate*, in the unit titled "Advanced reports.")
AC03S-3-3	Changing margins and page orientation (This objective is also covered in *Access 2003: Intermediate*, in the unit titled "Advanced reports.")
AC03S-3-5	Sorting records in tables, queries, forms and reports (This objective is also covered in the units titled "Fields and records," "Simple queries," and "Using forms.")
AC03S-4-2	Previewing for print
AC03S-4-2	Using datasheet, PivotChart, Web page and layout views (This objective is also covered in the unit titled "Databases and tables", as well as in *Access 2003: Intermediate*, in the units titled "PivotTables and PivotCharts" and "Internet integration.")
AC03S-4-3	Printing database objects and data

Explanation

Modifying a report

You can modify a report by opening it in Design view. For example, you can change a section's background color by changing its Back Color property. You can also do the following:

- Group records based on similar field values.
- Display the sum, average, minimum, and maximum values for each group or for every record.
- Sort or group the data by specific fields in a report.

Moving and resizing controls

You can change a report's appearance by changing the properties of the controls and sections in the report. You can also drag a control to a different place and resize it by using the resize handles.

Previewing the report

On the Report Design toolbar, click the Print Preview button to see how the report will look when printed.

7–16 Access 2003: Basic

Do it! **B-1: Modifying a report in Design view**

Here's how	Here's why
1 Click [icon]	(The View button is on the Report Design toolbar.) To switch to the report preview. The heading is not centered, and the values under all the columns are right-aligned.
2 Click [icon]	(The View button is on the Print Preview toolbar.) To switch to Design view. You'll modify the report's appearance.
3 In the Report Header section, edit qryOrderItem to read **Sales Details**	(Select the report heading, click inside the report heading box, and edit it.) To make the report's heading more meaningful.
Select the report heading as shown	[image of Report Header with "Sales Details"]
	(Click anywhere outside the report heading, and then select the report heading box.) This is a label control. When you select it, handles appear around the text, and the shape of the pointer changes to a hand. Now you can drag the report heading to another location in the Report Header section.
4 Drag the report heading to the center of the report	
5 In the Page Header section, select **Quantity**	Resize handles appear. Now, you can reduce the field heading Quantity to a suitable size.
6 Point to the left resize handle, as shown	[image showing Quantity with resize handle]
	A double-headed arrow appears.
Drag to the right as shown	[image showing Quantity resized]
	To reduce the size.
7 In the Page Header section, select **Product**	You'll change the heading.
Edit Product to read **Product ID**	To make the heading more meaningful.

Working with reports **7–17**

8	In the Detail section, select **sngItemQuantity**	You'll reduce the size.
	Drag the left resize handle to the right	
		To reduce the size of sngItemQuantity.
9	Reposition the objects as shown	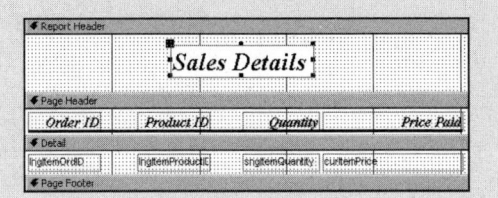
10	In the Detail section, select **lngItemOrdID**	
11	Click [icon]	(The Center button is on the Formatting toolbar.) The values in the field lngItemOrdID will be centered.
	Align the lngItemProductID field to center	Select the lngItemProductID label control, and click the Center button on the Formatting toolbar.
12	Click [icon]	(The Print Preview button is on the Report Design toolbar.) To preview the report.
	Observe the preview	
		The heading is now centered, and the field values are aligned.
13	Click **Close**	(The Close button is on the Print Preview toolbar.) To return to Design view.
14	Update the report	

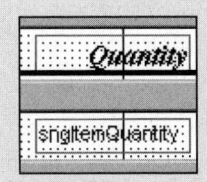

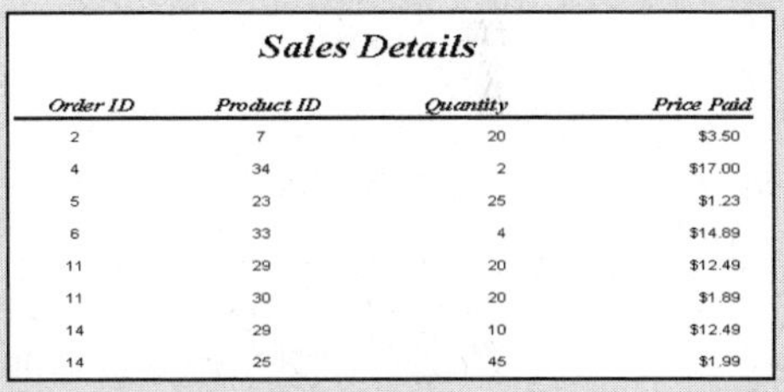

Grouping records in a report

Explanation

You can group records based on a specific field to display all the records for that field at the same time. For example, you can group data by Order ID to display all records with the same Order ID together in a report, as shown in Exhibit 7-4. You can place a group name above each group, or place a field showing a total or other calculated value at the end of each group.

Sales Details

Order ID	Product ID	Quantity	Price Paid
2	7	20	$3.50
4	34	2	$17.00
5	23	25	$1.23
6	33	4	$14.89
11	30	20	$1.89
11	29	20	$12.49
14	25	45	$1.99
14	29	10	$12.49

Exhibit 7-4: A report sorted and grouped on Order ID

Grouping and sorting records

To group and sort records, click the Sorting and Grouping button on the Report Design toolbar. In the upper pane of the Sorting and Grouping dialog box, specify the the sort order and the field by which you want to group the records, as shown in Exhibit 7-5.

In the Group Properties pane of the Sorting and Grouping dialog box, you can specify a Group Header or Group Footer. If you set any of these to Yes, a separate section for Group Header or Group Footer is introduced in report Design view, where you can place any information for a group of records.

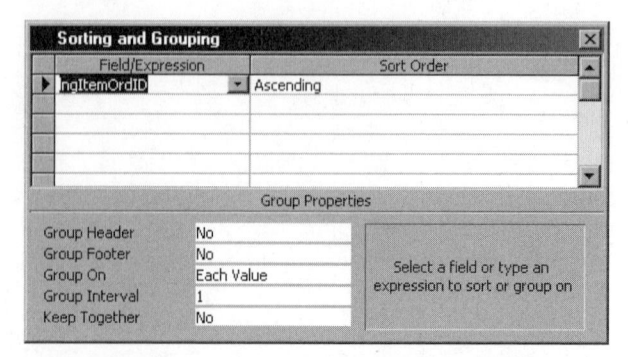

Exhibit 7-5: The Sorting and Grouping dialog box

Working with reports **7-19**

Do it!

B-2: Grouping information in a report

Here's how	Here's why
1 Click [icon]	(The Sorting and Grouping button is on the Report Design toolbar.) To open the Sorting and Grouping dialog box.
Observe the dialog box	The insertion point is in the first cell under Field/Expression.
2 From the Field/Expression list, select **lngItemOrdID**	You'll group records by lngItemOrdID.
3 In the Sort Order column, verify that Ascending is selected	To ensure that records are sorted in ascending order based on the values in the lngItemOrdID field.
4 In the Group Properties pane, click the Group Header box	A drop-down arrow appears.
From the list, select **Yes**	A Group Header section will be shown in Design view, where you can add information about the group. If you don't add anything to this section, a blank line will appear before each group.
5 Close the dialog box	
6 Click [icon]	(The View button is on the Report Design toolbar.) To view the report in Print Preview. The records are sorted in ascending order and are grouped based on the values in the field Order ID.
7 Click **Close**	To close the Print Preview window.
8 Update and close the report	
9 Close the query	

Error checking in reports

Explanation

While creating reports, you might make technical errors such as referring to a field that doesn't exist or trying to group or sort records in an invalid manner. Access provides an error-checking smart tag that identifies such errors in forms and reports. The smart tag displays the Smart Tag Actions menu. You can choose an option from the menu to correct the error.

Do it!

B-3: Checking errors in reports

Here's how	Here's why
1 Open rptRetailer in Design view	(Click the Reports button on the Objects bar, select rptRetailer, and click the Design button.) You'll check the smart tag for common errors in this report.
2 Place a text box control in the Detail section of the report	(A label control appears along with the text box control.) The text box control shows "unbound," indicating that the text box is not associated with any control source.
3 Display the property sheet for the text box control	(Press F4.) You'll associate an invalid control source with this text box.
4 On the Data tab, in the Control Source box, enter **Name**	To specify an invalid control source.
5 Close the property sheet	Notice that a smart tag appears next to the text box.
6 Click as shown	
	The Smart Tag Actions menu appears.
Observe the menu	Invalid Control Property: Control Source No Such Field in the Field List Edit the Control's Control Source Property Edit the Report's Record Source Property Help on This Error Ignore Error Error Checking Options...
	A number of options appear in the menu. You can choose any of these options. For example, you can choose the Ignore Error option to ignore the error.
Click anywhere on the report	To close the menu.
7 Close the report	Do not save the changes.

Adding summary information

Explanation

Calculated values for groups of records, such as totals and averages, are referred to as *summary operations*. You can add summarized data for a specific field by using either the Report Wizard or Design view.

To add a summary function in a report by using the Report Wizard:

1. Click New to open the New Report dialog box.
2. Select Report Wizard, and then select the table on which to base the report. Click OK.
3. In the first step of the Report Wizard, select the desired fields. Click Next.
4. Add a field to the grouping level, and click Next.
5. Specify the sort order. Click Summary Options to open the Summary Options dialog box, as shown in Exhibit 7-6.
6. In the dialog box, check the summary value you want to calculate.
7. Click OK to close the dialog box and return to the Report Wizard.

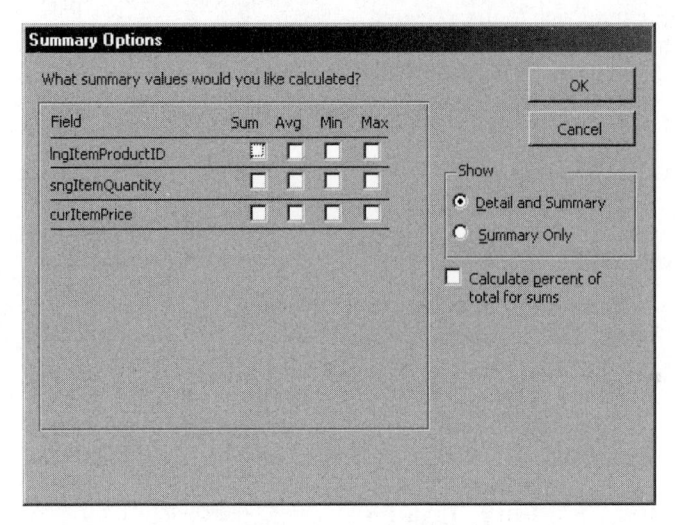

Exhibit 7-6: The Summary Options dialog box

Do it!

B-4: Adding summary fields by using the Report Wizard

Here's how	Here's why
1 Click **Reports**	(On the Objects bar.) If necessary.
2 Click **New**	To open the New Report dialog box.
3 Select **Report Wizard**	
4 From the drop-down list, select **tblOrderItem**	You'll create a report based on this table.
5 Click **OK**	To open the Report Wizard.
6 Move the fields lngItemOrdID, lngItemProductID, sngItemQuantity, and curItemPrice to the Selected Fields list	(Select the fields and click the Add button.) To move the selected fields from the Available Fields list to the Selected Fields list. You'll view these fields of the tblOrderItem table in the report.
7 Click **Next**	
Select **lngItemOrdID**	(If necessary.) You'll group records based on this field.
Click **>**	
Click **Next**	In this step, you can specify the field by which you want to sort the records.
8 From the first list, select **lngItemProductID**	You'll sort records by lngItemProductID.
Click **Summary Options...**	To open the Summary Options dialog box, as shown in Exhibit 7-6.
Under curItemPrice, check **Sum**	To calculate summary values for curItemPrice.
Under Show, verify that Detail and Summary is selected	
9 Click **OK**	To close the Summary Options dialog box and return to the Report Wizard.
10 Click **Next**	

Report layout and style

Explanation

The arrangement of data and labels in a report is referred to as its *layout*. When you create a report by using the Report Wizard, you can specify a layout and a style instead of using the Report Wizard's default layout and style.

To choose a report layout and style:

1. Select a layout for your report from the Report Wizard dialog box, as shown in Exhibit 7-7. The default page orientation is Portrait. Select the Landscape button to change the page orientation.
2. Click Next.
3. Select the desired style. Click Next.
4. Enter the title that you want to give your report.
5. Click Finish to preview the report.

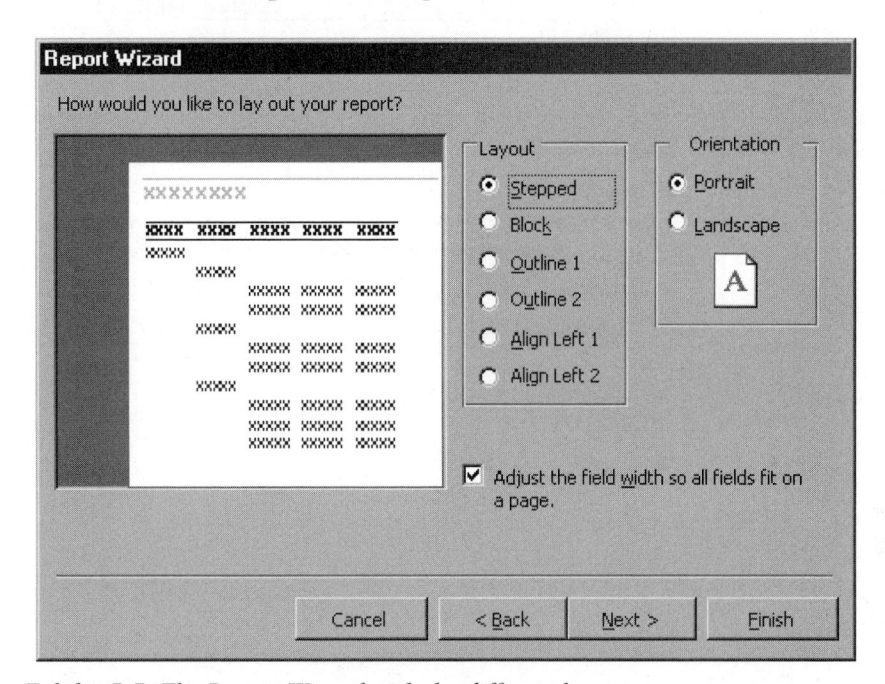

Exhibit 7-7: The Report Wizard with the different layouts

rptSummaryReport

lngItemOrdID 1

Product	Quantity	Price Paid
1	100	$3.00
11	50	$4.25
12	150	$5.50

Summary for 'lngItemOrdID' = 1 (3 detail records)
Sum $12.75

lngItemOrdID 2

Product	Quantity	Price Paid
3	400	$1.75
7	20	$3.50

Summary for 'lngItemOrdID' = 2 (2 detail records)
Sum $5.25

lngItemOrdID 3

Product	Quantity	Price Paid
5	200	$1.00

Exhibit 7-8: Preview of a report that appears at Step 10 of the following activity

Do it!

B-5: Modifying the layout and style of a report

Here's how	Here's why
1 Verify that the Report Wizard is open	
Observe the wizard	(Shown in Exhibit 7-7.) The current layout, Stepped, is the default layout.
2 Under Layout, select **Outline 1**	This will be the new report layout.
3 Under Orientation, verify that Portrait is selected	
4 Verify that Adjust the field width so all fields fit on a page is checked	
5 Click **Next**	
6 Select **Bold**	To specify the style.
7 Click **Next**	
8 Edit the What title do you want for your report? box to read **rptSummaryReport**	
9 Verify that Preview the report is selected	
10 Click **Finish**	You'll see a preview of the report, as shown in Exhibit 7-8. The total quantity sold to each customer appears in the preview.
11 Click **Close**	(The Close button is on the Print Preview toolbar.) To close the Preview window.

Access 2003: Basic

Explanation

Field properties

In a report, as in a form, each section has its own properties. You can change the properties of an entire section or specific fields.

To change the properties of a specific field, select the field in the Detail section of Design view, and click the Properties button on the Report Design toolbar to display the property sheet. You can change the property values by selecting and modifying the various options, such as Back Color, Special Effect, and Height. To see the effect of the changes you've made, close the property sheet.

Do it!

B-6: Changing field properties

Here's how	Here's why
1 Open rptSummaryReport in Design view	If necessary.
2 In the Detail section, select **curItemPrice**	You'll change the properties of this field.
3 Open the properties sheet	Press F4.
4 Click the **All** tab	If necessary.
5 Place the insertion point in the Back Color box	You'll change the background color of the field.
6 Click […]	The Color dialog box appears.
7 Select a shade of yellow	To change the background color to yellow.
8 Click **OK**	
9 In the Special Effect box, select **Raised**	You'll apply the raised effect to the field.
10 Select **sngItemQuantity**	You'll change the properties of this field.
11 Set Back Color to green, and set Special Effect to Raised	

12	Select **lngItemProductID**	
13	Set Back Color to blue, and set Special Effect to Raised	
	Close the properties sheet	
14	Change the title in the header to **Summary Report**	Click in the box to enter edit mode. The wizard made the title the same as the file name.
15	Click [icon]	(The Print Preview button is on the Report Design toolbar.) To preview the report. The fields appear in different colors.
16	Update the report	Choose File, Save.

Printing reports and other database objects

Explanation

You can print a report by clicking the Print button on the Report Design toolbar. You can also print a report by opening the Print dialog box, as shown in Exhibit 7-9, and clicking OK. To open the Print dialog box, choose File, Print or press Ctrl+P.

You use these same commands to print other types of database objects, such as tables, forms, and queries. To do so, simply open the object you want to print, and choose File, Print.

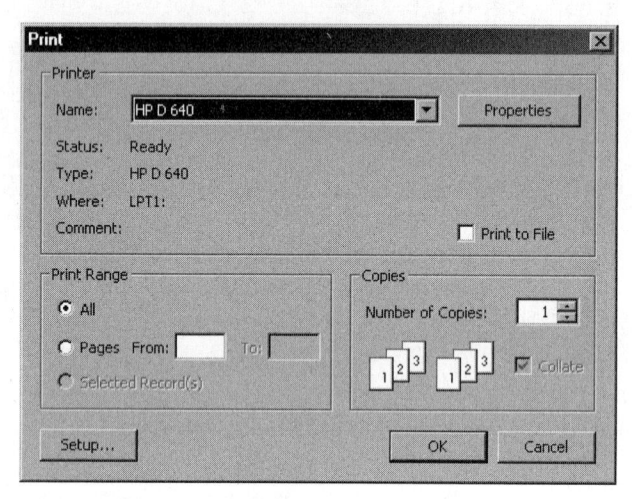

Exhibit 7-9: The Print dialog box

Do it!

B-7: Printing a report

Here's how	Here's why
1 Choose **File**, **Print...**	To open the Print dialog box
2 Verify that the default printer is selected	
3 Under Print Range, verify that All is selected	
4 Under Copies, in the Number of Copies box, verify that 1 is selected	
5 Click **Cancel**	To cancel printing.
6 Close the report	
7 Close the database	

Unit summary: Working with reports

Topic A In this topic, you created a report by using **AutoReport**. You learned that AutoReport creates reports that automatically contain all the fields from the source table. You created reports by using the **Report Wizard**. You learned that the Report Wizard guides you through every step of designing a report. You also created a report by using Design view and by using a **query**.

Topic B In this topic, you **modified a report** in Design view. You also **grouped** records and performed summary operations on the records in a report, by using the Report Wizard. In addition, you changed the properties of the fields in a report. You also learned how to select a style and a **layout** for a report. You also learned how to **print** a report.

Independent practice activity

1. Open CreateReportPractice.
2. Use AutoReport to create a report based on the table tblOrderItem.
3. Save the report as **rptReportPractice** and close the report.
4. Create a columnar report based on the query qryPractice.
5. Save the report as **rptSalesReport**.
6. Close the report and the query.
7. Using the Report Wizard, create a report based on the tblEmployee table. Use the following settings, and compare your report with Exhibit 7-10:

Item	Description
Display the fields	
Group the report by	
Sort in ascending order by	
Summarize by calculating the average (Avg) of	
Layout	
Title background color	
Specify title	

8 Change the background color of the Detail section (choose any color), and set the Special Effect property to Raised.

9 Preview the report.

10 Update and close the report.

11 Close the database.

12 Close Access.

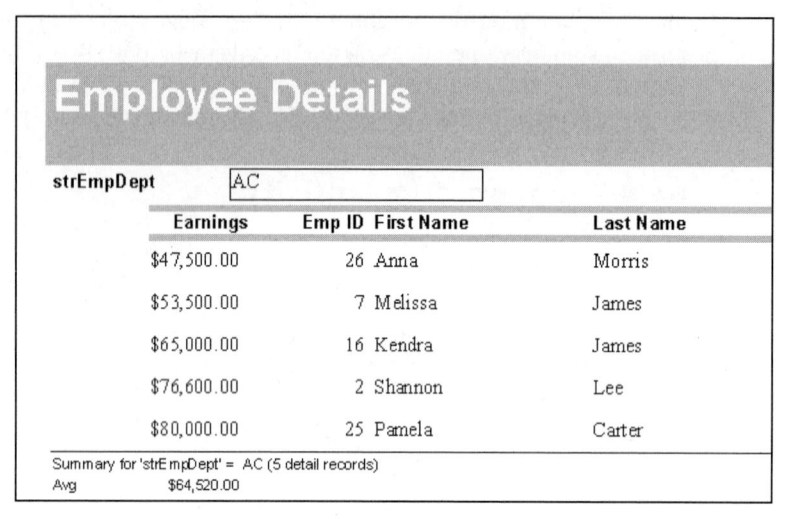

Exhibit 7-10: A sample of the Employee Details report after Step 7 of the Independent Practice Activity

Review questions

1 Name two ways to create a report.

2 How do you preview a report before printing it?

3 Which of the following is the default layout of a report that has been created by using AutoReport?

 A Columnar

 B Tabular

 C Portrait

 D Landscape

4 When creating a report, where do you specify the table or query that contains the source data?

5 What is the procedure to group and sort records in a report?

6 If you want to add total amounts to a report, what feature should you use?

7 Which of the following is not a layout option for a report?
   A Stepped
   B Block
   C Align Left
   D Centered

8 How do you change the properties of a specific field in a report?

9 Name one way to print a report.

Appendix A

Microsoft Office Specialist exam objectives map

This appendix covers this additional topic:

A Access 2003 Specialist exam objectives with references to corresponding coverage in Course ILT courseware.

Topic A: Comprehensive exam objectives

Explanation

The following table lists all Access 2003 Specialist exam objectives and provides references to the conceptual material and activities that teach each objective.

Objective	Course level	Conceptual information	Supporting activities
Creating databases using Database Wizard	Basic	Unit 2, Topic A, p 4	A-2
Creating blank databases	Basic	Unit 2, Topic A, p 7	A-3
Creating tables using Table Wizard	Basic	Unit 2, Topic C, pp 16-17	C-1
Modifying table properties or structure	Basic	Unit 2, Topic C, p 22 Unit 3, Topic A, pp 2-6	C-3 A-1, A-2, A-3
Creating Lookup fields	Intermediate	Unit 2, Topic A, p 2-3	A-1
Changing field types	Basic	Unit 2, Topic C, p 22 Unit 3, Topic A, p 4	C-3 A-2
Changing field properties to display input masks	Basic	Unit 4, Topic B, p 9	B-1, B-2
Modifying field properties for tables in Table Design view	Basic	Unit 4, Topic A, pp 2-7	A-1, A-2, A-3, A-4
Creating and modifying one-to-many relationship	Intermediate	Unit 1, Topic B, p 10 Unit 1, Topic C, p 17	B-2 C-3
Enforcing referential integrity in a one-to-many relationship	Intermediate	Unit 1, Topic C, pp 16-19	C-2, C-3, C-4, C-5
Creating and modifying Select queries using the Simple Query Wizard	Basic	Unit 5, Topic A, p 4	A-2
Creating and modifying Crosstab, unmatched and duplicates queries	Advanced	Unit 2, Topic A, pp 2-4	A-1, A-2
Creating forms using the Form Wizard	Basic	Unit 6, Topic B, p 9	B-1
Creating auto forms	Basic	Unit 6, Topic A, p 5	A-2
Modifying form properties	Basic	Unit 6, Topic C, p 17	C-4
Modifying specific form controls (e.g., text boxes, labels, bound controls)	Basic Intermediate	Unit 6, Topic C, p 14 Unit 2, Topic B, p 8 Unit 4, Topic A, p 2 Unit 4, Topic B, pp 6-8 Unit 4, Topic D, pp 14-17	C-2 B-2 A-1 B-1, B-2 D-2, D-3
Creating reports	Basic	Unit 7, Topic A, pp 5-13	A-2, A-3, A-4, A-5

Microsoft Office Specialist exam objectives map   A–3

Objective	Course level	Conceptual information	Supporting activities
Adding calculated controls to a report section	Intermediate	Unit 5, Topic B, pp 14-16	B-1, B-2
Creating data access pages using the Page Wizard	Intermediate	Unit 8, Topic B, pp 11-12	B-2
Entering records into a datasheet	Basic	Unit 2, Topic B, p 10 Unit 2, Topic C, p 26	B-2 C-6
Using navigation controls to move among records	Basic	Unit 2, Topic B, p 12	B-3
Importing structured data into tables	Advanced	Unit 4, Topic D, pp 17-18 Unit 5, Topic A, pp 2-4 Unit 5, Topic C, p 9 Unit 5, Topic E, p 19	D-1 A-1, A-2 C-1 E-1
Adding calculated fields to queries in Query Design view	Basic	Unit 5, Topic C, pp 21-22	C-5, C-6
	Intermediate	Unit 3, Topic B, pp 14, 17-18	B-1, B-3
Using aggregate functions in queries (e.g., AVG, COUNT)	Basic	Unit 5, Topic C, p 24	C-7
	Intermediate	Unit 3, Topic C, p 19	C-1
Aligning and spacing controls	Intermediate	Unit 4, Topic C, p 12	C-2
Showing and hiding headers and footers	Basic	Unit 6, Topic C, pp 12-13	C-1
Aligning, resizing and spacing controls	Basic	Unit 7, Topic B, p 15	B-1
	Intermediate	Unit 5, Topic A, p 4 Unit 5, Topic B, p 14	A-2 B-1
Changing margins and page orientation	Basic	Unit 7, Topic B, pp 23-24	B-5
	Intermediate	Unit 5, Topic C, p 19	C-2
Formatting a table or query for display	Intermediate	Unit 3, Topic B, p 16	B-2
Sorting records in tables, queries, forms and reports	Basic	Unit 3, Topic C, pp 12-14 Unit 5, Topic A, p 10 Unit 6, Topic D, p 24 Unit 7, Topic B, p 18	C-1, C-2 A-5 D-2 B-2
Filtering datasheets by form	Basic	Unit 3, Topic C, p 17 Unit 6, Topic D, p 25	C-4 D-3
Filtering datasheets by selection	Basic	Unit 3, Topic C, p 16	C-3
Identifying object dependencies	Advanced	Unit 5, Topic D, pp 14-16	D-1, D-2
Previewing for print	Basic	Unit 7, Topic A, pp 2-3 Unit 7, Topic B, p 15	A-1 B-1

Objective	Course level	Conceptual information	Supporting activities
Using datasheet, PivotChart, Web page and layout views	Basic	Unit 2, Topic B, pp 10-12 Unit 2, Topic C, pp 20-21 Unit 7, Topic B, pp 23-24	B-2, B-3 C-2 B-5
	Intermediate	Unit 7, Topic C, pp 10-11 Unit 8, Topic B, pp 6-7, 17-18	C-1 B-1, B-4
Printing database objects and data	Basic	Unit 7, Topic B, p 28	B-7
Exporting data from Access (e.g., Excel)	Advanced	Unit 4, Topic D, p 20	D-2
Backing up a database	Advanced	Unit 6, Topic A, p 11	A-5
Using Compact and Repair	Advanced	Unit 6, Topic A, p 10	A-4

Course summary

This summary contains information to help you bring the course to a successful conclusion. Using this information, you will be able to:

A Use the summary text to reinforce what you've learned in class.

B Determine the next courses in this series (if any), as well as any other resources that might help you continue to learn about Microsoft Access 2003.

Topic A: Course summary

Use the following summary text to reinforce what you've learned in class.

Unit summaries

Unit 1

In this unit, you learned that a **database** is used to store data in **tables**. You also learned about **fields** and **records**. Next, you learned how to **start Access**, and you examined the **Access window**. Then, you **opened a database** and examined the **Database window**. You also learned how to use **Help options** to get information on Access topics. Finally, you learned how to **close a database** and **close Access**.

Unit 2

In this unit, you learned how to create a database by using the **Database Wizard**. You learned about **Datasheet** and **Design** views for tables. Next, you created a table by using the **Table Wizard**. You also learned how to set the **primary key** and **add fields** in a table. Finally, you learned how to **save** a table and **add records** to it.

Unit 3

In this unit, you learned how to **modify a table** by **changing field names** and **deleting** and **inserting** fields. Next, you learned how to use the **Find and Replace** dialog box. You also learned how to **undo** changes in a table. Then, you learned how to use the **spelling checker**. Finally, you learned how to **sort** and **filter** records in a table.

Unit 4

In this unit, you learned how to set the **Required**, **AllowZeroLength**, **FieldSize**, and **SmartTags** properties. Next, you learned how to set **input masks** for fields by using the **Input Mask Wizard**. Then, you learned how to set the **DefaultValue**, **Validation Text**, and **Validation Rule** properties for a field. Finally, you learned how to set **single-field** and **multiple-field** indexes.

Unit 5

In this unit, you learned how to **plan** and **create** a **query**. You created queries by using the **Simple Query Wizard** and **Design view**. You also learned how to **sort** and **filter** records in a query result. Next, you **modified** the **values** in a query result. Finally, you learned how to use **comparison operators** and **calculated fields** in a query.

Unit 6

In this unit, you examined a **form** in **Design view**. Next, you created a form by using the **Form Wizard**. Then, you learned how to create a form in **Design view**, **add controls**, and **modify** the **properties** of controls. Finally, you learned how to use forms to **find**, **sort**, and **filter** records.

Unit 7

In this unit, you learned how to create a report by using **AutoReport**. You also created reports by using the **Report Wizard**, **Design view**, and **queries**. You also learned how to **group records** and **add summary information** in reports. Finally, you learned how to select a **layout** and **style** for a report.

Topic B: Continued learning after class

It is impossible to learn to use any software effectively in a single day. To get the most out of this class, you should begin working with Access 2003 to perform real tasks as soon as possible. Course Technology also offers resources for continued learning.

Next courses in this series

This is the first course in this series. The next courses in this series are:

- *Access 2003: Intermediate*
- *Access 2003: Advanced*
- *Access 2003: Application Development*
- *Access 2003: VBA Programming*

Other resources

For more information, visit www.course.com.

Access 2003: Basic

Quick reference

Button	Shortcut keys	Function
	CTRL + N	Displays the New File task pane.
		Indicates the current, or active, record.
		Indicates that you are in the process of editing the record but have not yet saved it.
		Indicates that you can enter data for a new record.
	Y	Moves the record selector to the next record.
	Z	Moves the record selector to the previous record.
	CTRL + ↓	Moves the record selector to the last record.
	CTRL + ↑	Moves the record selector to the first record.
	CTRL + +	Adds a new record.
		Switches to Design view.
		Sets a field as the primary key.
	CTRL + F	Finds a value in a table.
	CTRL + Z	Restores the previous value of a field.
		Opens the Indexes window.
		Runs a query.
		Totals the values in a field.
		Creates a form.

Button	Shortcut keys	Function
		Opens the toolbox.
B	CTRL + B	Makes selected text bold.
	F4	Opens the property sheet.
		Sorts records in ascending order.
		Filters records.
		Shows filtered records.
		Shows a form or report in Print Preview.
		Centers the selected text.
		Sorts and groups records.

Glossary

Aggregate functions
Used to calculate values for a group of records by adding the values to the Total row of the query design grid.

AllowZeroLength property
Used to specify that the field can contain null values.

AND comparison operator
Used to specify more than one condition in the criteria and display the records that satisfy all of the conditions.

AutoForm
A feature that generates a form that contains all of the fields of the source table, and then displays the form in Form view.

AutoReport
A feature that generates a report that contains all the fields of the source table, and then displays the report in Print Preview.

Bound controls
Controls that are linked to the fields of the underlying source table. Any change made in a bound control is reflected in the underlying data source. Text box controls are an example of bound controls.

Comparison operators
Used to add criteria to a query to view records based on multiple conditions.

Control
An object in a form that displays data, allows you to edit data, or performs some action.

Data value
An item of data.

Database
A collection of data, or information. An example of a simple database is a phone book that contains the names, phone numbers, and addresses of individuals and businesses.

Database management system (DBMS)
A set of programs used to store and organize data and to make data retrieval efficient.

Database toolbar
Contains buttons for frequently used actions, such as opening or saving a file. These buttons are shortcuts to some of the available commands in the menus.

Datasheet view
Displays data in a tabular format, containing rows and columns. Datasheet view helps you scroll through records and add, edit, or view data in a table.

DefaultValue property
Used to assign a default value for the field, even if nothing is entered in the field.

Design view
Gives you complete control over the table's structure. If you want to change the design of a table by adding or changing field details, you can do it in Design view.

Entity
Any object that has a distinct set of properties.

Expression
A combination of symbols—identifiers, operators, and values—that produces a result. An expression can include the normal arithmetic operators for addition (+), subtraction (-), multiplication (*), and division (/).

Field
A specific type of information or data value in a table.

FieldSize property
Used to specify the maximum number of characters that can be entered in the field.

File format
The specific format in which each application stores data. By default, Access 2003 creates databases in the Access 2000 file format.

Filter
A set of conditions applied to data to view a section of data.

Filtering
The process of temporarily isolating a subset of records that satisfy certain criteria you specify.

Form
An Access database object that allows you to view, edit, and add data to a table. The datasheet view of a table shows you a grid of fields and rows, while a form typically shows just one record at a time.

Form Wizard
A feature used to create a form that prompts you to select the fields to be included, the order in which the fields will appear, a layout, and a style for the form.

Format property
Used to specify the display format for data in a field.

Group
Used to organize database objects through shortcuts.

Handles
Small, black rectangles around a control. You change the size of a control by dragging the handles, and you move a control by dragging the whole control when the pointer changes to a hand.

Index
Used to arrange data in the ascending order of value in a field and to find data in tables. An index in Access is similar to the index of a book, which you use to locate information.

Input mask
Defines how data should be entered in a field, and also determines the type of data and the number of characters.

Input Mask Wizard
Used to create an input mask based on the built-in input masks in Access.

Layout
The arrangement of data and labels in a report.

Macro
Used to automate frequently performed database tasks, such as printing a set of weekly reports.

Menu
Contains commands to perform a set of related tasks.

Module
Used to automate and customize database operations. Modules are programs written in Visual Basic.

Multiple-field index
Based on two or more fields in a table, such as First Name and Last Name fields.

Null value
A value that indicates missing or unknown data in a field.

Objects bar
Located in the left pane of the Database window, it shows various database elements, or objects, such as tables, forms, and queries.

Office Assistant
An animated character that helps you interact with the Access Help feature.

OLE Object data type
Used to link to objects created in other applications, such as Microsoft Word.

OR comparison operator
Used to specify two conditions in the criteria and display the records that satisfy either of these conditions.

Page
Used to show table data on the Internet.

Pivot Chart view
Helps you display data graphically in Datasheet view.

Pivot Table view
Helps you analyze data.

Primary key
A field that uniquely identifies each record in a table.

Property inheritance propagation
The feature that enables you to update the properties of an existing object when the properties in the underlying table have been changed.

Property sheet
Used to change or customize the properties of a form control, such as Caption and Font Name. The property sheet contains five tabs: Format, Data, Event, Other, and All.

Query
A database object that retrieves data based on criteria from one or more tables and displays it.

Record selector
The small box to the left of each record in a table that is used to navigate through the records. The record selector points to the currently active record and indicates its status. The icon for the record selector changes based on the status of the record.

Relational database
Any database that uses an RDBMS to organize data. This database can have multiple tables that contain data about various entities, such as products, sales, or customers.

Relational database management system (RDBMS)
A type of DBMS in which data is organized in the form of related tables. In related tables, one or more fields are linked to fields in another table. This link ensures that you can enter only those values that have corresponding entries in the other table.

Record
A single set of related data values.

Report
An Access database object that presents data in an organized format suitable for viewing on screen or printing.

Report Wizard
A feature used to create a report that prompts you to select the fields you want to include in the report.

Required property
Used to specify a field that cannot contain null values. If the Required property is set to Yes, you must enter a value in the field.

Row selector
Indicates the active row with a black triangle in Design view.

Single-field index
Based on one field in a table. This index helps you find and sort data in tables that contain large amounts of data.

SmartTags property
Used to specify actions—such as sending e-mail, scheduling a meeting, or showing the calendar—for the data values in the fields.

Sorting
The process of organizing records in a meaningful way so that you can retrieve data in an order of your choice.

Source table
The underlying table containing the data that provides the field values in a form.

Spelling checker
A tool that uses a built-in dictionary to check the spelling of words.

Status bar
Located at the bottom of the window, it displays the current status of ongoing tasks.

Summary operations
Calculated values for groups of records, such as totals and averages. You can add summarized data for a specific field by using either the Report Wizard or Design view.

Table
A database object that consists of a collection of records that are used to store data.

Task pane
Located at the right side of the window, it contains shortcuts to frequently performed tasks.

Template
A pre-defined database structure provided by Access.

Title bar
Contains buttons you can use to change the window size or close the window.

Unbound controls
Stand-alone controls that do not have a data source. Use unbound controls to display information (such as labels), lines, rectangles, and pictures.

Validation rules
Used to check data that has been entered into a field and verify that it matches the conditions for the type of data, the data format, or the number of characters that can be entered in a field.

Validation Text property
Used to display a customized error message when the validation rule is not satisfied.

Wildcard operators
Used as placeholders when specifying criteria in query conditions to retrieve multiple values There are two frequently used wildcard operators: the question mark (?) and the asterisk (*). The question mark is used to substitute for a single character. The asterisk is used to substitute for any number of characters.

Index

A

Access window components, 1-4
Aggregate functions, 5-22, G-1
AND condition, 5-19
AutoForm, 6-5
AutoReport, 7-5, 7-13
Avg function, 5-24

C

Comparison operators, 5-16
Controls
    Adding, 6-16
    Bound vs. unbound, 6-5
    Defined, 6-5
    Label, 6-5
    Moving and resizing, 6-16
    Text box, 6-5
Count function, 5-24

D

Data types, 2-20
    Text, 2-22
Database
    Closing, 1-14
    Creating manually (blank database), 2-7
    Creating with the Database Wizard, 2-4
    Defined, 1-2
    Objects in, 1-8
    Opening, 1-6
    Planning, 2-2
    Relational, 1-3
    Rules for naming, 2-4
    Terminology, 1-2
Database toolbar, 1-4
Database window
    Components of, 1-7
    Toolbar, 1-7
Datasheet view, 2-8, 2-10, G-1
DBMS (Database management system), 1-2
DefaultValue property, 4-14
Design view, 2-8, G-1
    Creating forms in, 6-12
    Creating queries in, 5-6
    Creating tables in, 2-20
    For forms, 6-2
    For tables, 2-14
    Moving fields in, 3-6

E

Entity, defined, 1-3, G-1
Error checking in reports, 7-20
Expression, defined, 5-21

F

Field Properties pane, 2-14, 2-21
Fields
    Adding, 2-22
    Adding to queries, 5-13
    Calculated, 5-21
    Changing names of, 3-2
    Defined, 1-2
    Deleting, 3-4
    Deleting from queries, 5-14
    Inserting, 3-4
    Moving, 3-6
    Setting default values for, 4-14
    Setting properties for, 4-2
    Setting validation rules for, 4-15
File format, 1-6
Filter, defined, 5-2
Filtering
    Advanced Filter/Sort, 3-19
    Defined, 3-12, G-1
    Filter By Form, 3-17, 6-25
    Filter Excluding Selection, 3-18
    Query results, 5-11
Find and Replace, 3-7, 6-22
Form Design toolbar, 6-3
Form View toolbar, 6-24
Forms
    Adding titles to, 6-14
    Creating in Design view, 6-12
    Creating with AutoForm, 6-5
    Defined, 6-2
    Entering data in, 6-8
    In Design view, 6-2
    Navigating in, 6-7
    Section properties, 6-17
    Using to find records, 6-22
Functions
    Avg, 5-24
    Count, 5-24
    Max and Min, 5-22
    Sum, 5-22

H

Help
  Microsoft Access Help task pane, 1-11
  Office Assistant, 1-13
  Type a question for help box, 1-11

I

Index
  Defined, 4-18
  Multiple-field, 4-19, G-2
  Single-field, 4-18
Input mask
  Creating, 4-9
  Valid characters for, 4-10
InputMask property, 4-9

L

Label controls, 6-5
Literal characters, 4-9

M

Max function, 5-22
Microsoft Access Help task pane, 1-11
Min function, 5-22

N

Names
  For fields, 3-2
  Rules for, 2-4
Navigation buttons, 6-7
Null value, 4-2, 5-15

O

Objects
  In Access databases, 1-8
  Rules for naming, 2-4
Objects bar, 1-7
Office Assistant, 1-13
OR condition, 5-18

P

Pivot Chart view, 2-8
Pivot Table view, 2-8
Primary key, setting, 2-24
Properties
  DefaultValue, 4-14
  InputMask, 4-9
  Property inheritance propagation, 6-20
  Required, 4-2
  SmartTags, 4-7
  Validation Rule, 4-15
  Validation Text, 4-17

Q

Query
  Changing the design of, 5-13
  Creating in Design view, 5-6
  Creating with the Simple Query Wizard, 5-4
  Defined, 5-2
  Planning, 5-2
  Running, 5-9
  Saving, 5-9
  Searching for null values, 5-15
  Using an OR condition in, 5-18
  Using AND condition in, 5-19
  Using calculations in, 5-21
  Using comparison operators in, 5-16
  Using wildcard operators in, 5-20
Query Design toolbar, 5-9
Query results
  Editing, 5-12
  Filtering, 5-11
  Sorting, 5-10

R

RDBMS (Relational database management system), 1-3
Record selector, 2-12, 3-20
Records
  Defined, 1-2
  Deleting, 3-20
  Editing in query results, 5-12
  Filtering, 3-17, 3-18, 3-19
  Finding, 3-7
  Grouping in a query, 5-22
  Grouping in a report, 7-18
  Sorting, 3-12
  Undoing changes in, 3-9
  Using forms to find, 6-22
Report Design toolbar, 7-18
Reports
  Adding summary information, 7-21
  Checking errors in, 7-20
  Creating with AutoReport, 7-5
  Creating with the Report Wizard, 7-7
  Defined, 7-2, G-3
  Grouping records in, 7-18
  Modifying, 7-15
Required property, 4-2

S

SmartTags property, 4-7
Sorting
  Defined, 3-12
  Query results, 5-10
  Records in a table, 3-12
Source table, 6-2
Spelling checker, 3-10
Sum function, 5-22
Summary operations in reports, 7-21

Switchboard, definition, 2-6

T

Table
- Adding text fields to, 2-22
- Changing field names in, 3-2
- Creating in Design view, 2-20
- Creating with the Table Wizard, 2-16
- Defined, 1-2
- Deleting fields from, 3-4
- Finding records in, 3-7
- In Design view, 2-14
- Inserting fields, 3-4
- Opening, 1-10
- Saving, 2-25
- Setting primary key for, 2-24
- Source, 6-2
- Undoing changes in, 3-9

Text box controls, 6-5

Toolbar
- Database, 1-4
- Database window, 1-7
- Form Design, 6-3
- Form View, 6-24
- Query Design, 5-9
- Report Design, 7-18

Type a question for help box, 1-11

V

Validation Rule property, 4-15
Validation Text property, 4-17
Views
- Switching between Datasheet and Design view, 2-8
- Types of, 2-8, G-1

W

Wildcard operators, 5-20

Notes

Notes

Notes

Notes